REBOUND

REBOUND

by
K.C. Jones

with

Jack Warner

Quinlan Press
Boston

To my Mom, and to Ellen and to all my children.
K.C.

To Coach Bill Mogé — thanks for the memories.
Jack

ACKNOWLEDGEMENTS

We want to thank Beth Hanlon for making this book possible.

A few years ago a Great Celtic fan named Andy Meagher gave my son Chris a book entitled "The Picture History of the Boston Celtics." It's written by George Sullivan and published by Bobbs Merrill Company, Inc. The edition we have takes the reader through the 81/82 season. My respectful congratulations and thanks to Mister Sullivan for a wonderful job. The book was invaluable to us.

Also thanks to the noble Thomas 'Satch' Sanders, Steve Curly, M.L. Carr, Mildred Duggan, Kate Warner, and David Dupree of *USA Today*.

And of course the Trivia King and our friend, Boston Restaurateur, Bobby Hilson.

Mister Stephen Thompson of the Basketball Hall of Fame has all the answers to any basketball questions.

As usual, we couldn't have done it without Dennis Campbell of DMC Associates, Boston Ma.

Jack Warner
K.C. Jones

Introduction

I f you've ever been in the Boston Garden when the Celtics are playing, you know it can be a very noisy place. Other basketball teams have to stick to the rules and use five men, in the Garden the Celtics have the edge of an extra man—the intense encouragement from our fans is our sixth man.

I'll bet that anyone who has ever played or coached with the Celtics will agree that the instant when the team comes out on the floor and the sound of the fans' excitement and pride bursts over us and the hair stands up on the back of our necks is a memory we all store and cherish, and every once in a while, for the rest of our lives, we wish we could have that moment back just one more time. It's that good, believe me. Somewhere deep inside us, I'm sure all of us wish that our magic moments in Celtics life could have lasted forever. I have been lucky to have had more moments than most, but now I'm sure this kind of life won't last forever.

Right now, I'm not in the Boston Garden, the crowd is much bigger, and the sound creates an even greater thrill in my belly and up my back. Through the rolling roar of the crowd's noise I hear the police officer with the starspangled collar tell Mayor Ray Flynn that the Department has an estimate of the crowd's size.

"How many?" asks the Mayor.

"We figure over a million and a half at the parade, Mr. Mayor."

"Wow," says the Mayor.

"And we figure over two hundred and fifty thousand down there," the cop adds, pointing down at the sea of faces below us.

Mercy! I thought as I stood on the balcony of Boston City Hall and looked down at the endless jam of smiling, shouting, cheering people. When I stepped to the microphones, a huge, happy, rolling tidal wave of sound rose up to me. I stood there for a brief moment as images of Hitler, Mussolini and Evita flashed through my mind. They had this strong, strong stuff more than once. This could get you off balance, could make you forget who you really are.

I was going to be speaking as the coach of the World Champion Boston Celtics professional basketball team, and the thought hit me with as much power and force as the cheers of the crowd. Less than five years ago, when I was looking for a head coaching job in the NBA, I couldn't get people to return my phone calls. Nobody in the world of basketball had time for me. It hurt to know the pros had given up on me.

After being fired in Washington with a winning record, I reached out for every pro job that came up. The best I could manage was to get an interview for a job with the Chicago Bulls. They decided to stay with their own, while everybody else in professional basketball ignored me. There was more pain in store when I discovered that even the colleges had no time for me. Some of the names of the colleges on the West Coast, the Midwest, the South, and the Northeast—even here in Boston—rippled across my mind. Those colleges hadn't had the time to answer a letter or a phone call, much less, give me an interview. Now I was about to say a few words to hundreds of thousands of people who had taken the day off to come here to congratulate the Celtics for winning the championship and me for having coached this team. What a turn of events. It's mah-ve-lous. But I'm not going to lose my balance—I did that once.

T his year's championship ring will be sweeter than all the others I've received. Someone in the media said that no one else has earned as many winning basketball awards in as many different ways. I have two NCAA championship rings; I am proud to have an Olympic Gold Medal for basketball; and I've recieved eleven NBA championship rings. I earned one as an assistant coach of the Los Angles Lakers and the others as a player, assistant coach and coach of the Celtics. This may be unique—I don't know. But I do know that all the winning doesn't mean that it's been easy. Along the way I had to learn to deal with losing before I was able to win again.

There are going to be some people out there whose jaws will drop when they see that I got myself involved with a book— particularly any of my former classmates. But things change for all of us. The sea coast takes on a different look, the mountains get worn down, some people's hair turns grey and K.C. has his name on a book. Lord knows this is something I never expected, but then I really never expected to have the kind of life I've had so far.

I suppose there are a number of reasons for getting invloved in this project, and I hope that if you stay with me to the last page you will understand them better. I do know that one of the buttons that got pushed that motivated me to get involved in this project is a story I heard a while ago.

It seems the owner of an NBA superpower was looking for a new head coach for his team. One of the candidates he interviewed—who is still an NBA coach—began to explain his approach to coaching pro basketball by telling the owner that the winning pro team requires specific talents. First, the team needed a monster center who can dominate the defense by blocking shots and rebounding and who also has a good shot. Second, the team must have at least one great shooter. Third, he said, there must be a superb ball handler to bring the ball up the court and get it into the hands of the monster center or the great shooter or the next best shooter. This ball handler must be able to penetrate with the ball so that he disrupts the other team's defense.

The coach listed two or three other specialties that his team must have because, he said, that the owner must understand that all professional athletes are idiots. He said they are brainless robots that must be told exactly what to do and when and where to do it.

The owner reacted to the coach's remarks with surprise, and suggested that what he meant to say was that some professional athletes are "limited." He pointed out that former professional athletes are sitting in the U.S. Congress and on the Supreme Court, so they can't all be stupid.

"No," the coach said, "I meant what I said."

It seems strange to me that a man who earns his living in professional sports would say the kind of thing that echoes the attitude of too many fans and casual observers—an attitude that is resented by those of us who have played sports. Any coach who regards his players as a group of well-trained thoroughbreds with the brains bred out of them is making one hell of a mistake. I learned early that a leader who has no respect for his followers will never receive any long term respect from them. I also learned that there are some quiet points of view that need airing, and that's one reason I chose this forum to express my own perspective.

In order to understand what I mean it would help to look at the context of my life—a life that's had it's share of struggles, confrontations, joys and achievements, and not all revolved around the sport of basketball.

What began as a childhood pleasure and a college delight became a profession. As I say that word I pause. I'm not sure I ever thought about it this way, but it's true. My profession is basketball. For almost thirty years I've gone to work in front of a lot of people. I've done it with men who put their reputations on the line night after night to cheers or boos; men of intelligence and sensitivity who have publicly succeeded or failed at the work they do. We tasted victory or fell on our faces in the press and in front of our families, our friends and often on TV with millions of Americans watching. That's the world I live in, the world of professional basketball. I admire most of the men who have shared this world with me—and became close friends with some of them.

This story will be a mix of my memories, of battles on and off the court, defeats and victories of the past and present and of the wonderful people whose lives were enriched by all of that. It will also be the story of a personal defeat that hurt more than anything that ever happened to me on a basketball court.

I think the best way to begin is with this year—the 1985-1986 National Basketball Association season. Let's see where it takes us.

REBOUND

Chapter One

It's Thursday, the 26th of September. The summer went by so fast I didn't even see it—too many basketball camps, too many appearances scheduled. The summer's pace was so hectic that it's almost—almost—easier doing what puts the real bread on the table—coaching the Celtics. Training camp starts tomorrow, so today my assistants, Jimmy Rodgers and Chris Ford, and I spent most of our time making sure we feel comfortable with our plans for tomorrow, pre-season and the season.

The first day of training camp is going to be different this year. We're going to begin with a media day. We'll go out to the country club in Hingham and play golf and tennis and relax. We'll have an easy, loose day together. I want the players to interact with each other and get that Celtics family feeling bubbling before the hard work begins. The radio and TV news reports are talking about a major storm approaching New England. We have one coming too—it's called pre-season practice.

Jimmy and Chris are at the blackboard writing suggestions a mile a minute for training camp. They're both good, bright guys who make a lot of sense. I'm sitting and watching and listening while part of my mind goes over some of the other items on the pre-season agenda we have to stress. First, of course, we have to get everybody in shape. That's not a serious problem with our guys. They're pros. They know you've got to be able to run that court constantly. It's up to me to give them enough work to be in shape by the time the season starts.

I remember my pal Willie Naulls coming to us years ago after being a star with the Knicks and almost passing out during his first practice session. He was dragged off the court by his heels. Our vets know we start off with long, hard up and down the court running. They're prepared or else. The rookies learn this right away.

Last year we were actually a better team than the championship team of the year before, but we didn't win the championship. The difference was injuries. We've got to fine tune this year's team and hope that Mr. Injury doesn't come knocking at our door.

My thoughts suddenly focus on the word aggressive. Like the aggression I saw last year in the faces of the Lakers, especially Mitch Kupchek and Kurt Rambis—great players, highly aggressive, highly motivated with a single purpose. To win in every situation. Of course, we had just gone through gang fights and wrestling matches with Cleveland and Detroit—the really hard-nosed physical stuff that our division has that the Lakers don't see much of out West.

Last year they seemed to have held a good deal of their aggressive energy in reserve, after a superb season under their great coaching strategist, Pat Riley. They were caught off guard only momentarily in that first classic game in the Garden where we registered a sound defeat. But like true champions, they came back with a vengeance and our energy level had been sorely tested.

I've got to make sure our people don't let this happen again. Aggressive play means every one of our guys has to understand his role on the team—for the team. We've got talent, no doubt about it, but the league is full of talent. We have the most important element—the confidence of being on top. We're a team that has won sixty games or more a year. It takes a special kind of character to be on top like that and to maintain that consistency. We've done that very well in the last four or five years.

My goal this year is to do a better all around coaching job and yet not take away from the players' creativity. These players aren't robots, but some things must be automatic. The discipline for that required automatic response will come through the repetition of training camp. One of the things that Jimmy and Chris and I will try to accomplish in camp is to make certain parts of the game so automatic that the players will react in pressured situations without having to do any panicked thinking. I suppose that's what military discipline is all about. You get in a tense situation and the old automatic reflex takes over. For us it's a different kind of war with different kinds of weapons. In basketball the most important offensive weapon we have is the fast break and it must be automatic. Rebound—pass out and up the court. Always up the court, on the run before the enemy can get dug in. Everybody on the Celtics has to run. Each of the front three men takes a lane that consists of one third of the width of the court. It's got to be automatically at full—under control—speed. The only way anybody can avoid using the fast break is to find some guy twelve feet tall and toss the ball to him. Otherwise the fast break is the answer to eliminating the other guys' height or defensive advantages.

The thought of defense turns my mind to that aspect of the game that is so important and so often neglected by teams who are dominated by players who think that their great shooting and scoring are their contribution to the team and that everybody ought to be grateful to them for not lying down and taking a nap when the other guys have the ball. That's not the Celtics way. It wasn't my way when I was playing, and it will never be our team's approach to the game. We will work hard to have a disciplined defensive attitude. Everyone must be quick to come over and help out his teammate when the other team has a player who's giving us fits and is a handful for whoever is playing him.

So, on this September afternoon my mind is full of basketball—as usual. My two assistants are chalking away on the blackboard while my thoughts are on the year ahead—a year that can be a great one if we put it all together. I guess by "all," I mean applying the right amount of each of the following: discipline, freedom, imagination, aggressive selflessness and, of course, being physically fit and injury free.

W ell, the first day of camp and our big plans for a happy-go-lucky media day have been blown away by a very aggressive lady named "Gloria." There are lots of stories about why hurricanes are named after women but I'll leave those to all the funny weathermen to tell. Right now I am disappointed and so are the players. The storm has wiped out the golf and tennis tournaments. The television and radio interviews have been cancelled. Everybody is at home and waiting for the storm to hit.

I was looking forward to this day because it creates the kind of situations that I believe help mold a team. The guys would be together, yakkety yakking, hitting the golf ball a little bit and kidding around. Larry, Kevin, Danny and Dennis all like to joke around.

Dennis has just signed a big contract and is feeling good about that. He should. He deserves it. He likes to be with people and I would guess that would be especially true now that he has become an acknowledged star. I'm sure those guys are sorry to miss this day. I wanted to have Parish play a little tennis. Even though Robert's seven feet tall he could have a pretty good serve. This social activity is important to me as a coach. I want the players to be as relaxed as possible so they will establish a good flowing rapport with one another. As they get to know one another, the next step they reach will be mutual respect.

It is vital for a team that the players really get to know each other and have a good time with one another. Once the game starts they carry that attitude onto the court. They show that respect, that understanding that it takes to help a good or great talent become a better or greater talent. If players feel comfortable with one another, they are more apt to allow each other the freedom to perform at their best, which is also the freedom to make an occasional mistake while trying to be creative. Even if the coach encourages creativity, it can only happen if a player's teammates allow that atmosphere to flourish. Trust and respect for fellow teammates bring more success than all the X's and O's that were ever chalked on a blackboard.

Hurricane Gloria put a damper on this day but only the day. Hopefully my ideas will be put together through the season.

The media is having a field day with the storm. For them to be fulfilled something has to be happening. The hurricane gives them a happening that touches everybody. I'm listening to the radio and they're giving out "toot toots" and warning everybody, giving a play-by-play account of the storm's progress as it comes up from the Carolinas. It's almost like a pregame talk to all of New England. The families are the players and the media is the coach saying "Do this, do that, get ready." We run around buying up all the food in the local stores—all the flashlight batteries, ice, canned goods. It's like game time, but now we're preparing for a dangerous game.

Fears begin to build up that this storm's force could knock the house down. Not just trees, the house. My daughter Holly and Christopher, my two year old, are sticking close to me. I understand—it's a scary time. The closer the storm gets, the bigger the imagination makes it.

Finally, Hurricane Gloria arrives and the trees really shake and twist. I look out the window at our bird bath, which is a heavy, sizeable thing, and I wonder if the wind could blow it around. Suddenly it crosses my mind that the house probably is not insured for this kind of storm. I'm not certain of that but I sure will find out. I think of the upcoming season and of how many variables there are to winning a championship. Injuries are one large factor, and there is no insurance to compensate. We learned this fact last year.

The main thrust of the storm was supposed to hit around two or three o'clock in the afternoon. Right about then, after too much watching and waiting, Christopher fell asleep. Holly, bored by now, was also dozing. My wife Ellen and I decided there was a message there. We went upstairs to try resting ourselves. Ellen had been up most of the night before with Christopher so the minute her head hit the pillow she was asleep. I lay there looking out the window watching the trees, hoping the roof would stay on the house. The electricity is out so I can't watch any game videos. Would I analyze basketball games in the middle of a hurricane? No—but I can use the time to think of some game strategies to take my mind off the storm. And I do.

W e've had some good practice time under our belts and September has just gone. We are very close to picking the final roster. In the next week we will give the rookies and a couple of the old-timers an even closer look so that we can make our evaluation where there is a little uncertainty and have as few question marks as possible. My goal is to start the season with a team that is in sync and can make beautiful music together.

Chapter Two

This is the roster I'm looking at right now.

1985—1986 Boston Celtics' Roster (#1)

No.	Name	Pos.	Hgt.	Wgt.	Birthdate	College	Yrs.Pro
44	Danny Ainge	G	6-5	185	3/17/59	Brigham Young '81	4
43	Andre Battle	G	6-3	195	8/30/63	Loyola Illinois '85	R-3 (70)
33	Larry Bird	F	6-9	220	12/7/56	Indiana State '79	6
28	Quinn Buckner	G	6-3	190	8/20/54	Indiana '76	9
42	Albert Butts	F	6-9	215	12/11/60	LaSalle '85	R-5 (116)
34	Rick Carlisle	G	6-5	207	10/27/59	Virginia '84	1
30	M.L. Carr	G-F	6-6	210	1/9/51	Guilford '73	9
40	Carlos Clark	G	6-4	209	8/10/60	Mississippi '83	2
3	Dennis Johnson	G	6-4	202	9/18/54	Pepperdine '76	9
50	Greg Kite	C	6-11	250	8/5/61	Brigham Young '83	2
12	Ralph Lewis	F	6-6	200	3/28/63	LaSalle '85	R-6 (139)
31	Cedric Maxwell	F	6-8	217	11/21/55	U.N.C. Charlotte '77	8
32	Kevin McHale	F-C	6-10	225	12/19/57	Minnesota '80	5
00	Robert Parish	C	7-½	230	8/30/53	Centenary '76	9
35	Chris Remley	F	6-8	215	11/23/62	Rutgers '85	R-7 (162)
11	Sam Vincent	G	6-2	185	5/18/63	Michigan State '85	R-1 (20)
41	Cliff Webber	F	6-8	235	8/10/63	Liberty Baptist '85	R-4 (93)
8	Scott Wedman	F	6-7	220	7/29/52	Colorado '74	11

Head Coach—K.C. Jones San Francisco '56
Assistant Coaches—Jimmy Rodgers Iowa '65
Chris Ford Villanova '72

Scout—Ed Badger   Iowa '53
Trainer—Ray Melchiorre   Bethel College '70

These are some of my thoughts as my eyes work down the roster list.

Danny Ainge—A veteran player who is one of the fastest players in professional basketball. I expect him to develop complete confidence in his shot this year. For the last few years teams have tended to let him take the outside shot figuring his lack of consistency is a weakness in our game. This year I look for Danny to be making that shot and I'm sure he will. Danny came to our rookie camp. That tells you something about Danny Ainge and the Celtics. Danny is a veteran with a nice contract. He could have been out on the golf course. He could have been at the beach, but there he was with the rookies working his butt off, working constantly on his outside shooting. Not because it makes Danny Ainge a bigger star but because he knows that it makes the team stronger. Danny's effort is above and beyond what most players in the league would be willing to do, but he knows that improving himself improves the team and eliminates an edge that other teams think they have on us.

As I think about the effort our guys put into their game it becomes only clearer to me that one of the so-called secrets of basketball is no secret at all. People like Danny Ainge and especially Larry Bird rise to the top because of pure hard work. Sure, you say Danny Ainge can run like a deer, has great hands, wonderful athletic skills. Larry Bird is 6'9", a magnificent shooter, and has a cool head and great God-given instincts for basketball. Those things can be said about most of the players who come into our league. The difference is the hard work that accompanies their brains. And make no mistakes about it, they are very smart. And they're tough. In fact, a few of these guys might have made the old Celtics teams that I played on! On the other hand, there are lots of lazy players in the NBA. They come in with a skill level that never improves. This is not the case with any player on the Celtics team. Each Celtic works hard and long to improve the skills he has and to add new ones. That's what Danny's doing right now. I watch his shot and I realize that, as it does in basketball after lots of hard work, suddenly like magic—pow—pow—pow—it happens. The man's shot is there. I believe it is all going to come together for Danny this year.

When we learned that Seattle wanted Gerald Henderson, it seemed like a God-sent situation. We'd had Gerald and Danny splitting the job at guard, which is like being quarterback in pro football. It was as though we were playing one quarterback in the first half and one in the second. Neither the man nor the team had a sense of who was in charge. Neither was getting enough playing minutes and their minds weren't right. Neither was completely fulfilling his role. Gerald had played great basketball for the Celtics but Seattle wanted him badly enough to offer a good draft pick. He is starting for Seattle and is an even better player now because he has the show.

The situation is similar here for Danny. Believe it or not, Danny is actually 6'5" but, for some reason he looks more like 5'6" out on the court. But he is 6'5" and he does it all. He hustles and scraps on the defensive end, and runs like the wind on the fast break. And now with Danny's outside shot working, I believe this year the opposing NBA teams will confront a player whose game is almost totally together. I say almost because I want him to add one more thing to his game when he's become totally confident of his outside shot. He must drive to the hoop. Take the ball in. When that becomes the final addition to his game—Mercy! Watch out NBA!

Here's the name Andre Battle. I see the name and I think about a phenomenon that puzzles me a great deal. I watched Andre in camp and his responses were so similar to those of so many rookies. They are not at ease. This surprises me.

You begin playing basketball in sandlots where you learn the tough way, from the Bible. You have no coach. You have to stand in line to get on the court. When you get on the court you have to win, otherwise you have an hour's wait to get back on again.

Then comes high school. You get yourself a name. You've got the cheerleaders and the girls. You're playing basketball and life is sweet. Then it's college and you're a hoop star. The opponents are big and tough and fast but you're as good or better than they are. A big team and an entire college are behind you, supporting you. But all of this is basketball. A ball and a hoop just like the sandlot.

By college a player should have a real sense of confidence when he walks out on that court. Yet, when the rookies drafted by the Boston Celtics arrive at camp, they're more nervous than I expect. It bothers me. I went through the same levels of experience but I knew it was still the same sport. I was one of those guys who couldn't put the ball in the hoop and everybody knew it. When I came to my rookie camp I knew I was going to scrap and hustle and fight every minute because no matter who the players were it was still basketball and I knew basketball. I wish the rookies who come to us could sense that.

Andre Battle came to us as a great shooter. To a certain extent he is, but not much else. His ball handling wasn't impressive. His favorite thing was shooting the ball. That's the best part of his game—

shooting. But he missed a lot. Maybe he was nervous. But either he had to get hot—hit three or four shots in a row—or he was out of business.

Ahh—Larry Bird. He is having trouble with his back. I can tell that it is really bothering him. We've got to have him healthy or it will be a very long season. Last year he suffered injury after injury. He slides across the court for the ball, dives over chairs. Superstars don't do that or fight like savages for an offensive rebound. Larry does and I know he always will.

Larry is 6'9". He is an average giant. I'm not sure most fans appreciate the energy Larry expends in every minute of every game that he is on the court. He never stops pushing out for rebounds. He crashes both boards. He is almost always in position to rebound whether it is offensive or defensive, and that requires unbelievable energy. First the man has to get down the court, then jump in the air for the ball and when he comes down he runs the length of the court on the fast break. Larry believes in the fast break. He knows how to get out on the wings instantly and if he doesn't get the ball, he is on the offensive boards. He may have just gone 180 feet in that run. Think of it. Larry is a big guy, jumping up and down, pushing out in the other direction, racing down the court, blocking the shot, making the quick pass, staying ahead of every play. It's ironic that the guards who are supposed to be the fast guys spend most of the game going from foul line to foul line. That's about sixty feet. Larry is running past those guys all night long, and while he is expending all that energy he is excelling at passing and shooting. He is the heartbeat of the Celtics team and has to be injury free.

Last year in the playoffs the index and pinky fingers of Larry's right hand were hurt. Each time they got hit it compounded the situation. He also had an elbow that was extremely painful. I don't think another player in the game, especially if he was a superstar, would have or could have continued to play with those injuries the way Larry did in the playoffs. Other players with less motivation would be sitting home nursing their wounds. Larry may hang on to the ball too long sometimes. He may take a shot that he wishes he hadn't taken. He may throw away a pass, but when Larry throws away a pass it's because he's trying to make a pass that few other players could even imagine. His bad passes are better than most other players' good ones. He has so much confidence, he'll try anything on the court. If it doesn't work, he'll try something else. Nobody else can do what Larry can do and nobody else works as hard at doing it. He is the finest basketball player alive and he's one of the smartest men—young or old—I ever met. He's got a special wisdom.

Quinn Buckner—He has a great knowledge of the game. He'll do anything you ask of him. When you talk to him he concentrates totally on what you say, with those big eyes laying right on you. You watch him on the court and you can believe he is an ex-linebacker in football. He plays the game the way I played it. Grouchy. Always after the ball. Bugging this guy here, nagging that guy there. Helping out where he can, doing whatever needs to be done. His brains and his imagination are always right on top of the game. His only problem is that sometimes the whole thing doesn't seem to mesh physically. He is a great team player and there is no question in my mind that he has a future as a coach. I am also sure that Quinn could do very well in business. As far as basketball goes, a problem we have to solve with him is his shot. He is a better shooter than I was—but I only shot nineteen percent. He has no qualms about taking the shot and I like that about him. The problem seems to be when he should take the shot. We have discussed this and I hope that we can work it out because he certainly wants to do whatever is best for the team.

Allan Buttes—He is a guy, 6'9", from LaSalle. He has a nice touch but he hasn't shown me what he does best. He hasn't shown any fundamentals out there. He's got this long slim body that could get out and streak and hustle, but he isn't very active. If a player can't scrap, then he has to show me that he is a great outside shooter or a great something. I just haven't seen any of that from Buttes.

His Dad called me up to see how I felt. I told him much of the same as I'm saying here. I suggested that if he wants to impress a coach, impress him with hustle and scrap. If a player's shots aren't going in, then he can always give that fighting battle for a rebound. That never hurts. But Buttes just hasn't yet shown me any of those required abilities. No real scrap in him.

Rick Carlisle—He's the psychologist on the team. A very bright youngster. Very confident. Two years ago he made this team just from watching what went on out there. Rookies in training camp play second fiddle to the first round draft pick. A rookie figures, well, I want to make the team but first draft takes that. But second and third and fourth and on down the line—I get to beat them—everyone of them. You look at them and you try to give the team something they can't give.

What I'm looking for in rookie camp is what the players do best and how they execute the rest of the game. Players who don't have the talent—shooting, shot blocking or moving, pushing the ball up the court—have to show me hustle and scrap. Darien Drakes with the

Bullets I coached years ago made the team just on hustle and scrap.

If you want to impress a pro coach, let the guy know you are having fun. Let the coach know that if you miss your shot, you're the first one back on defense. If there is a loose ball, be the first one to get it. Always be in position. If it's an offensive board, be in position to get the ball. If you lose the ball, then you go the other way—fast. When the other team scores you jump out of bounds to get the ball into your hands to make that quick pass or be the first one down the court. Either way you are looking to help your teammates. That's a player. If he has some talent to go with this drive, then the player has something going.

Rick Carlisle always has his eyes on the ball. When he handles it, people come running to double team him. They think he's awkward but they don't get the ball away from him because he's a very fine ball handler. He is smart on the court as well as off the court. This past summer on his own initiative he played in a summer league. He wanted to improve his game. He was very intense about getting his spot on the team and he is just as intense about keeping it.

Carlisle had to take a back seat to this year's first round pick, Sam Vincent, but he hasn't sulked. He continues to play hard. That really impresses any coach, particularly me. Carlisle has been there working out in practice, doing everything he can. He doesn't like it when he's not in there full time. He gets irritated. Then he deals with it—never complains. He goes in and he performs. He does his job. He's probably not happy seeing Vincent here—the number one draft pick—another guard with a different style, but he understands that we need this type of player. Rick Carlisle will shoot from the outside or drop it off and set a nice pick. He is a little shaky on the defensive end—that's uncertainty in his mind. What he has to do is learn position on the man he's guarding. He will then be a very good defensive player. He's a smart player—he uses his head. Added to that is the other factor that I look for—he is a team oriented guy.

M.L. Carr has decided to retire. This is a sad, sad development. In his six years of performance, he gave the Celtics exactly what the Celtics are all about—pride, teamwork, joviaIness. If you can't have fun with each other and you withdraw into little groups, then you don't have a team. You won't be successful. You may win—but success lasts longer than winning. M.L. will be greatly missed by the rest of the guys. We want to keep him in the organization in some capacity.

Carlos Clark—He has a great touch. Looks super up in the air with his shot. He's quick and he's got great physical attributes—6'4" and a strong, strong body. He played forward in college. I don't think, however, he has a strong sense of fundamentals. Last year in rookie camp he just stepped in, going through the motions, three or four times then all of a sudden he started to come around. I recognized him when he started scraping, fighting on the boards. So, he made it through to rookie camp. He was on.

Funny, it doesn't seem right but it almost always happens, you know who is going to make the squad in the first three days of training camp. The players come and tell me themselves if they are going to make it. Carlos Clark did it in two days. So we brought him in. I don't know about this year. He's missing that required level of determination. He could shoot with Larry but he doesn't have Larry's fight. Not to use just Larry as an example. Clark just doesn't seem to have the scrap now.

Dennis Johnson—He has impressed me with his growth as a professional player this year. He always takes pride in himself. He is very jovial. Nothing gets past him. He's bright but he doesn't say much—just laughs and lets others talk. He is also very sensitive. I've never seen a player like Dennis. If an opposing player upsets him, it just brings out the best in him.

Dennis gave Blackman, from Dallas, a compliment. He said, "Gee you're great and a hell of a player and I hope you have a good year."

Blackman said, "Well, I'm not really playing very good right now but I'm gonna start killing everybody when I get in shape."

Dennis was giving the guy a compliment and the guy didn't accept it. Dennis went into the game and did a job on him. Dennis is a very sensitive fellow who usually keeps his emotions under control.

Dennis and I once had an experience that could have become a very serious concern. I learned an important coaching lesson and I wouldn't be surprised if Dennis learned from the experience too. During a practice session I criticized something that Dennis had done on the court. I repeated the criticism as the players stood around watching and listening. His attitude as I spoke caused me to ask him a question, "Do we have a problem here?"

We wound up in a very heavy argument and I told Dennis that if I was wrong about this I would apologize and that we should both think things over. The next day before practice we had a quiet talk. He apologized and I apologized, and it all worked out for the best.

The incident with Dennis taught me something—or re-taught me. I have done enough coaching to be aware of it and I shouldn't have had to be reminded forcefully—Don't strongly criticize a player in front of the others. Take him off to the other end of the court or another room and quietly make your point. This is particularly important in the pros. Believe it or not, we're more sensitive than college or high school players.

Dennis will be a real leader this year. He has just signed an excellent contract and he deserved every bit of it. He earns his money. He gets upset when practice is sloppy or if the guys are fooling during their drills. He's also made suggestions to other players. Sometimes he can do this much better than I can. That's how we used to deal with team-mates when I was playing. Dennis is really taking a step up—he is now a team leader, a key to our continued success.

It seems a strange thing about this team, but like all the great Celtics teams before, we have more than one person we can't do without. Over the years we've never had the league's highest scorer or highest anything, except for Bill Russell who surely was the best rebounder. The great Celtics teams have been made up of guys like Dennis Johnson who each brings a certain special sound to the music we make.

Greg Kite—He is not really appreciated by the media or the fans. They say he's just being kept on the team because he is a "heavy." This is not true. He's quick and a good rebounder. He's got bulk, smarts and scrap. When Moses comes down and wants to post up and you've got his spot, Moses is going to push you out. It helps to be 6'11", 250 pounds. Moses Malone doesn't push Greg around—no one does. We're going to use him to remind people of that and in the Celtic tradition he will give every bit, all the time without complaint. Greg is a team man who accepts his role.

Kevin McHale—It's amazing the way we got the long lean Irishman from Minnesota. Swapping draft picks had left us in sad shape, but as the third round pick came to our number—Bang! There's Kevin still available. Celtics luck? I wouldn't argue. McHale is a bright person. He loves to read. He loves basketball and loves to play the game. He loves to have a lot of fun too—to joke and fool around. He is not a very seri-ous practice person. He likes to put the ball in the hoop, get an offen-sive rebound. He majors in what he does best—working down low and getting the offensive rebound. He'll run and do everything else required of him.

Kevin loves to talk. We'll have stretching exercises and he and Dennis really work at it—without really working at all. I'll say, "Hands up in the air, turn your head." Kevin will be walking around with his hands up in the air, turning his head and talking all the time. He walks around when we do stretching. You have to stretch the achilles before you get into hard running, get the muscles warmed up. We'll be stretching and getting a little sweat—that means the body is warmed and everything is together. Kevin is out there and he may talk to eleven guys before the stretching is over. If we are sitting on the floor he'll scoot over and talk to someone. He says that's the Irish in him. If he's not talking he'll just lay on his back with his hands behind his head and his knees up. He'll just sit there. But that's the way he is and I go along with it. What is important is important—what's not important is not important.

Robert Parish—He is the Ray Berry on the team. He doesn't say much but he plays the game hard with both his mind and his body. For blocking shots he is the main man. He is the one with the big steals. In such tension-filled times as the playoffs he is a marvel with the big rebounds, the big blocks, and the big shots—that's amazing to me. Robert is so quiet until a clutch time in the game and suddenly he gets the rebound from the big people. He knows when the game is on the line and he's been doing this all along. He can be unappreciated all through a game—especially a big game—and then bang! He turns things around.

Robert is a classy individual. You'll hear that from players on other teams as well as from anybody else. With Larry and Kevin, Robert takes the back seat in the shots department. Kevin will get sixteen or seventeen shots and maybe more. Larry will get twenty-five shots, and Robert will only have eight or nine. I asked Robert if it bothers him and he said, "Coach, as long as we're winning." I expected him to say it bothered him quite a bit. That's why the Celtics have been so successful—because of this outlook. Someone has to sacrifice. You have five superstars out there and you may have one sitting on the bench. The other players are fine talents too.

Most superstars need to show their wares, to demonstrate their talent, creativity, and imagination. Sometimes this means a star's attitude will be, "Well, if he's getting twenty shots, I want to get twenty shots." All this comes into play around contract time. This is a money game—big money. Talents have a way of being competitive against each other or the team. You see it a lot in the league. But the Celtics players have a way of dealing with each other. These guys have this outlook and approach, which is the major reason why we are on the level we are—the highest level. We've been up there in the one or two spot for twenty-two or twenty-three years because of this attitude. If Robert didn't have the right mind set, we'd be in trouble. He is very special and all the guys, including the coaching staff, know that.

Chris Remley—He hasn't shown me much. He hasn't shown scrap. During the draft I had a spot for him. We needed someone in that small court spot and we were so far down the list in the draft that we knew we wouldn't get some of the best shots, so we took the next best—Remley. He showed something; that's how he got here in the first place. But we draft on what these guys did in college, on how they performed there.

In the draft we were looking for a shooting guard. The rest was more or less locked up. When we're drafting though, who knows? A player might be a fifteenth draft pick and we only go ten, but the guy might show something and he's been passed up.

Sam Vincent—Tremendous talent, tremendous confidence. He really impressed me. He has a great shot. He is a natural fast break guy. He comes down, re-forms and then drops it off. In a half court game he can penetrate. Once he begins to unite that with becoming a student of the game, he is going to be awesome. He looks slow out there but the man is fast. Just fluid. To look at him he's a little guy and doesn't look like much. He's Jay Vincent's brother and Jay looks the same—only Jay is 6'6" and Sam is 6'2". He started off with an uneven attitude. My impression was that he felt he was owed something because he was first round pick and he gave that impression when he came here. He made quite a big splash with the media. When he didn't get the minutes he expected in the exhibition games, he would stand off by himself leaning against a wall. He became very quiet and as soon as practice was over he was out—just change his clothes and in five minutes he was gone. I guess he was letting me know that I hadn't even let him work up a sweat.

In Detroit Sam had his whole family at the game and he got in the last two minutes of the last quarter. We already had a twenty-five point lead. He was terribly disappointed. Really down. Down to the point where he may have been thinking about giving it all up. I decided to call him in after that game and ask him about it. What I said in effect was, "You're not owed minutes here—you earn minutes. You have teammates you have to go out and be with and play with, you have to show them that you respect them. We have Larry Bird—we've got about five good guards including you here. You have to work your way up. You have to learn in practice. You have to learn the plays and you can't keep repeating the same mistakes on the offensive end."

Our conversation became a kind of confrontation. He had something important to say. He said, "Well, I'm out there and I'm trying to get experience." I understood that he was disappointed in not getting playing time, but I said that with the Celtics very few rookies walk right in to the starting five. I told him that he'd have to pay his dues with hard practice and constant work. I hope that our talk did something. He was smiling the next day. I think he felt better that he got things off his chest. If I did my job right, I got my point across. I want him to understand that despite the playing time he is most important to us. We want him to be part of the Celtics future. He can demonstrate to me that he wants that during the course of this year.

Cliff Webber—He's a nice shooter. He just isn't showing me enough get up and go. Not enough scrap and hustle.

Scott Wedman—Fire the ball up. Get him open and he'll put the ball in. He's 6'7" and looks more like 6'4". But he's the guy who boxes out and does all the fundamental things. Often the fans don't notice him out there. I notice him. He's like a wonderful piece of jewelry that isn't flashy. Some people forget that he was an All Star player at Cleveland and he deserved to be. He was one of the league's good forwards. For us he'll play forward, guard or drive the bus if we need it. He is a vital part of our team. When he came here and was getting twelve minutes or no minutes, he came up to me and said, "Case, can we talk?" He said, "I know that Larry and Kevin and Max have to get their time and I want you to know that whatever you want me to do, wherever I can help—forward or guard—I'll do it and you know I'll be ready. I want to help the team in any way I can."

Other players with his talent would be saying, "Trade me, I'm not getting any time. I'm gonna call my agent." But Scott Wedman, again like Robert Parish, has the right attitude, and that's a very important reason why we are on the level that we are. Of all the players on the team, Scott would not accept a trade. He can't do anything but be successful with that attitude. That's the Carlisles and the Wedmans. And Greg Kite who says, "Coach, whatever you need." Those are your bench people.

While I am in the middle of reviewing this roster, something very important has happened to our ball club. After weeks of talk, Cedric Maxwell has been traded to the Los Angeles Clippers for one of the legends of basketball—Bill Walton.

Bill has arrived in pretty good shape and we have put him right to work. He is a highly motivated perfectionist. He has great intensity and enthusiasm. He can do it all. Great passer and rebounder. His rebounding is a thing of beauty. When you see it, it's similar to a great shooter going up and shooting in slow motion. He has perfect timing. When the ball touches his hands and before he hits the floor, he already knows who is going to be open for the outlet pass. I've never seen anyone in basketball do that the way he can. No matter where that rebound is, when Walton gets it he knows what he's going to do with it before he hits the floor. He is probably the best big-man passer in basketball. Right now he tends to get a bit carried away and tries to do too much at the offensive end. But I'm sure that will work itself out.

And by the way—the man can shoot! If he stays healthy, he will be a tremendous asset to our team.

Apparently I mentioned the business of his getting a little carried away on offense to some of the reporters because *The New York Times* carried that story. I was sorry to read it because I believe very strongly that a coach should never criticize his players publicly, and since the story didn't say that I added I was sure that it would work itself out, it came across as public criticism. That night Bill hung around after everyone else had left. I knew he had something on his mind, that he wanted to talk to me. So I told him to come over. I asked if he wanted to have a talk and he said, "Yes."

He said, "Coach, you know, I played ten minutes in the last ball-game and I played nine minutes in this one. Now, there is nothing wrong with that, I'm not upset about that, but if you are mad at me—let me know. If you're not mad at me, I have no problem because I don't want to lose my job."

This from a legend. UCLA, championship after championship, an undefeated season. He leads a team when he's healthy. He led a team to an NBA title. But he has a history of injuries. He's had some destructive injuries. Anyone else in that same position would not be playing today. He's practicing and playing hard every minute and he tells me he's afraid of losing his job. Mercy! What a treat to have him with us.

One of the newspaper writers asked, "How do you feel about having Bill Walton on the team?"

What are you going to say to that question? "Well, I'm very happy about it," and try to keep from laughing with delight. But it's important to understand that we don't usually get players like Bill on the team because the other teams need them. The other teams won't release such talent. But the situation developed where we had a chance to get him. That kind of situation happens once in a lifetime—for him and for us—and if it works the way it can, this could be a year of great memories.

"Is he happy here?" someone else asked me.

Very much so. His nose was broken twice and he got bumped in the teeth in our first visit to Detroit. Yet, he has not missed a practice. In our next series he got an elbow in the mouth and a chipped tooth when he got a rebound. I took him out of the game. They called the team dentist. Has your dentist ever injected a needle up in the bony part of your mouth? Painful. Bill went back in the game after they did that to him. I went through the same thing years ago and I didn't move for two days. I stayed in the hotel, and I didn't get out of bed. Yet Bill

Walton came out and played.

So, we've got new personnel and Bill is a most valuable acquisition. He's a great passer—a great player. As I sit here, part of my mind considers Bill Walton. How are we going to fit him in? How important it is that he and Robert Parish go together and complement one another? I know Bill called Robert while our negotiations to acquire him were going on. He talked with him about their roles with the team and how he understood Robert was the number one man at the center spot. That communication shows what a smart, sensible professional Bill is. He wanted to be sure that he and Robert were on the same wave length before he came to the Celtics. He understands one of the game's fundamental rules: to be a winning team in basketball it's got to be a together team. It must be a happy family. It has to be a group of guys in harmony—making good music. Bill knows that. He and Robert have to be in tune making the same kind of music if they're going to be sharing the center spot and be winners.

Trading Max adds a bit of sadness to all of this. Max had some great days with the Celtics. He may find they are days that will look better and better as time goes on. I wish him luck.

Chapter Three

That's our roster and from this group of seventeen we have to narrow the number down to twelve. I should amend that— rather than seventeen we have eighteen. Number eighteen is a fellow named David Dupree who is a sportswriter for *USA Today*, the new nationwide newspaper. He contacted us and asked if he could participate in the pre-season workouts so that he could write a piece about it. Red and I talked it over and decided that since he had some experience as a player at the University of Washington, and because I felt that it might be fun for the fans to read about practicing and playing with the Celtics, we would let him spend a week with us. David, whom I knew from my Washington Bullets days, established a warm, easy relationship with the players that enabled him to catch some of the essence of what it is like to be part of the Celtics family.

He stayed with us and practiced with the team for a week of hard work and finished by playing briefly in an exhibition game with the Philadelphia 76ers. In his article, he explained the difference between our games and our practices. I guess you could say that the games are like a family all dressed up going to church on Sunday. Everybody is on their best behavior, smiling, putting their best face out to the world. Practices are the family sitting around the supper table. There's just the family,and you see it and hear it like it is. Dupree had that privilege and he grabbed it. I liked reading his piece because it gave me a fan's view, and although sportswriters would never admit it, there is a little or a lot of fan in all of them.

It might be interesting to explain how I run a practice. Perhaps the best way is to give you honest impressions as written by the sports-writer-basketball fan, David Dupree.

Think of Dupree as an honest to God rookie on the present Celtics team and taste some of the meal he sat down to with us. Here's the rookie's impressions of Celtics camp—

The routine in pre-season—up at seven-thirty, at the gym by eight-thirty. Get your ankles taped everyday and no matter how jammed the trainer's room, you're on the court in time or you're fined.   The gear hangs on a big safety pin—a jersey, reversible green and white, a pair of shorts, two pairs of socks, t-shirt, jock. There are two sets. The dirty gear goes back on the pin and thrown in a basket.

Formal practice from ten until twelve. Lunch break. Back to the gym at two-thirty. Get retaped. Practice five-thirty to six-thirty.

First minutes in the gym—old pros and stars, Scott Wedman, Dennis Johnson and star of stars, Larry Bird, come over and introduce themselves and welcome all the rookies. One by one, every one of the regulars does this in a very friendly way. Classy, absolutely. Suddenly we are not strangers and the rookies relax.

They really work during the time spent on stretching exercises. Every muscle gets stretched and it continues until the players break a sweat. It's serious business laced with some very funny wisecracks, but it is always intense. One amazing fact after stretching, it's quickly obvious these guys want to win at everything. The foul shooting, one-on-one, three-on-two, the scrimmages. They want to win. Not one of them is a gracious loser.

The occasional remark, obviously never to be forgotten, that they lost last year's championship.

The running—we run, run, run, run, run. That's the coach's style and, of course, it's also a Celtics tradition.

Everybody is bigger, stronger and quicker than you expected.

The constant three-on-three shooting games followed by endless three on two fast break drills.

The wisecracks that smooth the practice grind. Larry Bird missing a shot and muttering, "I hate this game."

Hearing Dennis Johnson, a nice blend of humor and total dedication to productive practice, say, "When in doubt, get the ball to Larry."

Kevin McHale puffing his way up the court, "I thought I could get in shape by switching from Coors to Coors Light. I was wrong."

Robert Parish, a charmer, not the stoic Chief the public sees, kidding Greg Kite, "The Mormon assassin."

Danny Ainge with his unbelievable athletic ability, the team cheerleader, always encouraging his teammates.

The thoughtful and determined Scott Wedman, who only eats natural foods and doesn't even drink tap water.

Rick Carlisle, hard working, intense, "They like intelligent team players here."

Bill Walton, pushing his body as hard as he can to overcome his years of injuries and doing it with the delight of a kid.

And always, Larry Bird, asleep on the mats in the gym at eight-thirty in the morning. Did he practice all night? Maybe. His play in a scrimmage that draws quick Ahs of respect and yelps of pleasure from his teammates. His wonderful grin as he does his thing, so much better than anybody else.

The coach stopping practice and quietly telling the rookie that he is playing too conservatively because he is afraid to make a mistake.

The repitition, walking through plays, running through it with no defense, running through it with a passive defense, running through it with a full speed defense. Simple plays, run over and over with options that come from the basic play.

Unlike other teams, the guards are expected to know the system so well that any of them can be a point guard.

The coach watches everything. When he speaks, it's always in a quiet voice. Everyone pays attention. Surprise when the coach asks the players their opinions on what the team is trying to do.

And finally, before the rookie's first game, the words of wisdom from the great Mr. Bird, "This ain't no time to be scared. Remember you ain't got no friends on the other team. All of your friends are right here."

The rookie is impressed by all of this. He should be impressed but not scared. It is life with the Celtics.

E very coach is different. I'm sure we all try to use what we think are the best things we've learned as we've followed the bouncing ball. This is not a book about how to be a basketball coach, but if I were a plumber talking about my life, you'd expect to hear something about plumbing, and if I weren't a basketball coach, I don't think you'd be reading the book.

So, I will talk about what you could call my philosophy of coaching, which is a reflection of my philosophy of life. What I've learned about coaching and what I've learned about life, I learned the hard way—mostly by making mistakes. I think I'm finally beginning to make fewer of them.

When I stopped practice and told the rookie, sportswriter, basketball fan, David Dupree that he was playing too conservatively, I was giving him a message about a mistake too many young players make. Basketball, like life, is a game of confidence, and you must have enough confidence to risk making a mistake. You cannot be timid and play good basketball. Fear of failing at a dribble, a pass, sometimes a shot, keeps many talented players from achieving the full development of their potential. I see it in some pro-players who are weak in a certain area and seem to be afraid to practice that particular skill over and over until they develop that skill because that practice means making mistakes or failing. They won't do it. They're afraid of failing, so they can never do a particular thing in a game. Opponents get to know that weakness and use it against the man.

Having enough confidence to make an occasional mistake is important in the development of a good basketball player. You must have a belief in yourself that's strong enough to let you fail in public and come right back and try again. Learning that lesson cost me an important part of my life.

The "rookie" was surprised that we expect both guards on the court to know the system so well that either one can call the play and act as point guard. That may not sound like a big deal, but not too many teams do that. Basketball fans who watch us play take it for granted. However, our approach tells something important about our belief in the team. I expect, and the team expects that the other guard who is not bringing the ball up the court and showing his fancy wares to the crowd, will not get his nose out of joint. He will accept his tempoarily reduced role and keep right on banging.

The "rookie" was surprised when I asked the players how they felt about a particular play, or a move, or an option. So are veterans who come to us from other teams. But I want the players to know that I don't think they're robots. I don't worry about anybody questioning who the boss is. That will take care of itself if I'm doing my job. I try to treat the players and the assistant coaches as equals. As a black man, and during some of the time in my career as an assistant coach, I learned too well that low down feeling of being ignored. You know they say that whale crap—pardon the expression—is the lowest thing in the ocean and, therefore, the lowest thing in the world. Well, there have been times when I've had to look up to see if there was any around. I don't want this to happen to any of the people on my team. I want our people to know that I respect their feelings and opinions on what we're doing. These men have great talent, and some of them are blessed with terrific imaginations. It's a mistake not to draw on this resource. A team will suffer with a coach whose ego gets in the way of the team. The only stars on the Celtics should be the players.

The day to cut the roster down to twelve has arrived. I've talked endlessly with general manager Jan Volk, and with Jimmy and Chris and, of course, I've have talked with Red who knows more basketball than the four of us put together. But now it's up to me. I'm the coach and my career will be affected just like the rest of these guys—in fact more than most of them—by the harmony this years Celtics squad achieves.

Naturally, certain new players don't have to worry. We've just acquired Jerry Sichting, a fine player, from the Indiana Pacers. He fills a need for us that other teams are aware of and have taken advantage of—that same need that has Danny Ainge working so hard on his shot. Jerry is a wonderful outside shooter. If other teams give us the outside shot this year, he'll take it and we expect he'll make it. So, Bill Walton and Jerry Sichting are part of this squad. With Max gone we've lost a regular who had been through the wars with us, a player of great personality and talent.

All of us will miss Quinn Buckner. He was traded to Indiana as part of the Sichting deal. Quinn is a great guy, a great team man, and a real scrapper. We hope Jerry Sichting will give us that same scrap and quickness, with the addition of a great shooting touch that Quinn — like me—unfortunately didn't have. One of the many reasons that I hated to see Quinn go was that he reminded me of myself.

Sly Williams has come to us with what I guess the media calls a "troubled history." As far as we're concerned, he is a great talent and will give us additional strength as a big forward on the boards at both ends of the court, where he really works hard, and with his shot, which is a good one. He'll provide back-up strength to Larry, Scott and, in a sense, Kevin. I talked with Sly before we got him from Atlanta. I told him that I consider him a star and a player of great talent who would be a starter anywhere else but on this Celtics team. I told him that he should realize that he will be getting less than twenty, twenty-five minutes a game with us and that he should think about that fact and be prepared to fill the role of a big forward coming off the bench, crashing the boards and making those quick, smooth passes that are one of his trademarks. Sly has played well in practice and exhibition games and will be on the squad.

Sam Vincent, our number one draft pick, has shown me that he has great potential and he will be on the squad.

The difficult decision I have to make is between two fine people and marvelous athletes. Rick Carlisle and David Thirdkill. I am already reading and hearing that the media and the public are watching this decision closely because it has come down to a question of a black player or a white player. Rick and David are individual players who do different things and fill different roles on the team. For me the decision is not going to be a hard one. David is a quick, strong player who has fine defensive skills. He plays hard, he practices well and he is a team player in the Celtics tradition.

Rick continues to be a very smart basketball player who watches closely and uses what he sees. He can bring the ball up and maybe because of his size fifteen flippers, he looks a bit awkward; other teams feel they can double team him and take the ball away from him. Nobody's done it yet. He has a wonderful outside shot which will only get better as his minutes and confidence increase. He has experience with us and I know he will do whatever is necessary to help the team without complaint. His attitude couldn't be better. So, as I hear more and more rumbling in the media, I am making my decision, which is really not a hard one, and the black and white issue is not a factor with me. The team is—and for the team I am going to keep Rick Carlisle.

So, here's the roster we start the season with.

No.	Name	Pos.	Hgt.	Wgt.	Birthdate	College	Yrs.Pro
44	Danny Ainge	G	6-5	185	3/17/59	Brigham Young '81	4
33	Larry Bird	F	6-9	220	12/7/56	Indiana State '79	6
34	Rick Carlisle	G	6-5	207	10/27/59	Virginia '84	1
3	Dennis Johnson	G	6-4	202	9/18/54	Pepperdine '76	9
50	Greg Kite	C	6-11	250	8/5/61	Brigham Young '83	2
32	Kevin McHale	F-C	6-10	225	12/19/57	Minnesota '80	5
00	Robert Parish	C	7-½	230	8/30/53	Centenary '76	9
12	Jerry Sichting	G	6-1	180	11/29/56	Purdue '79	5
11	Sam Vincent	G	6-2	185	5/18/63	Michigan State '85	R
5	Bill Walton	C	6-11	235	11/5/52	UCLA '74	11
8	Scott Wedman	F	6-7	220	7/29/52	Colorado '74	11
35	Sly Williams	F	6-7	215	1/26/58	Rhode Island '80	6

Chapter Four

It seems I may have underestimated the response to the Carlisle/Thirdkill decision, based on some newspaper reports that Thirdkill got an unfair shake. I know all too well that some of the press would maximize a story of racial problems on the Celtics, as a contrast to the years of Celtics' successes that emphasized blacks and whites playing and living with real camaraderie.

I am not going to be panicked into some kind of dramatic over-reaction simply because of some second-guessing by people who are not a part of the situation.

I was down in the South End today getting my hair cut at Foggy's. I've been getting my ears lowered there for years. Foggy is a good guy and he's been around Boston even longer than I have. Something that happened there reminded me that the black-white thing can cut both ways. Even the best of people can get hung up on it.

Foggy was puttering around, snipping away, the place was full of guys and they're all talking basketball and what kind of year the Celtics will have. Foggy, with a little grin on his face but a bit of an edge to his voice, says, "Well, you know if they ain't gonna have no black players—maybe they ain't gonna need a black coach."

All the guys sitting around the shop chuckled. As I sat there with this group of black people, I thought to myself, "How strange it is that I am being criticized or at least needled by black people for keeping a white player in preference to one of their own." The world has certainly taken some strange turns for me since those days of growing up in Taylor, Texas.

I grew up in the Jim Crow South. When I look at a confident young rookie like our Sam Vincent who is having real trouble with the amount of minutes he's getting, I wonder if he could even imagine living with separate restrooms, bubblers, restaurants, hotels, with sitting in a separate colored section at the movie house and taking his rides in the back of the bus. The odds against black people seemed as large as a mountain in those days.

I went to school for the first time when I was seven years old. My first day was an experience I've never forgotten. I didn't know how to read. Books were not part of our life. Sometimes we didn't have enough food, so getting a square meal had much higher priority than reading. As I look back, I realize we almost never had a newspaper, never mind a book. I remember being called on to read aloud my first day of school. I stood up and gave it my best shot — going very slowly, trying to make sure I pronounced the words the right way. Suddenly, the teacher interrupted me and told me to go home. She said I didn't know what I was doing, that I should come back next year. Talk about rejection! I walked around with my ears down like a rabbit for a long time after that experience. From that day on I never talked much either at home or any place else.

As far as my home goes, when I look back now I realize that what we were doing was surviving. We never sat around actually starving; on special occasions there would be chicken and meat, but often there were slim pickings of macaroni or beans or greens. Those days also taught me something about being a man in the middle. We slept three in a bed and the man in the middle doesn't have an easy time.

My father, whose name was also K.C. (just initials is the way we were baptized), was a hard working man. He worked in an auto plant and as a cook. He took jobs where ever he could find them and they were never easy to find. I remember my father as being very verbal, an outgoing musical man with much talent. He used to sing and play the guitar in church. I can recall watching my father hum and strum, putting his foot on the kitchen chair and playing his guitar. I'm sure I get my own love for music from my father. Even then I liked music enough to have the courage to stand up in church and sing with a quartet. I started doing that when I was six years old. Growing up it was the only time I wasn't afraid to open my mouth.

My mother, Eula, was a very different character than my father, which I suppose bears out the axiom of opposites attracting. She was inward, a very quiet person. She taught me that love carries more weight in action than with words. Her days were long ones, raising five children and working part-time as a maid. As the eldest I suppose

I didn't get what the experts call quality time, but I sure knew she loved me.

Regarding grandparents and great grandparents, I don't have considerable information. What I do have, however, has always intrigued me. I find that most Americans get a little hazy when they get into the great grandparent department. Often times it seems that we black Americans are even hazier on that part of our history. I do know that two of my great grandparents were Cherokee and Cheyenne Indians, and to top off that heritage, another was a German Jew. One thing is certain, whatever was put in the mix before I came along, I have been black since I was born. For those of you who have not had that experience, I can tell you truly that it doesn't make life easier.

I watched my mother and father work hard and search constantly for jobs to support us. They struggled to feed us, to put clothes on us and to keep a dry roof over our heads. We wandered across the heart of Texas through the depression years as my Mom and Dad looked for work. When I was two, we left Taylor for Corpus Christi. When I was four, we went to Dallas. When I hit the ripe old age of nine, we were in MacGregor, Texas.

We were a black family struggling to live in a white man's world. Nothing was easy for us. Early on I realized that white folks made the rules—all the rules. We didn't see ourselves as second class citizens. We didn't see ourselves as citizens. We didn't vote or ever think about the political world; it was beyond us. Washington, the State House or City Hall, we hardly knew they existed. That was the white man's place where he ran things. I hated the atmosphere that I saw. I knew what my father meant when I'd hear him say, "If you're black, step back."

I was the oldest and I tried to do what I could to help. I'd cook, I'd clean house and do what was necessary. Just keeping up with life on a daily basis was challenge enough in those days.

As far as the cooking goes it was something I learned to love. I was the family's main cook until I went away to college. Thanksgiving and Christmas were my days to shine. I'd stay up all night working away at the stove—enjoying every minute of it. I'd make a sweet potato pie, chocolate layer cake, I'd put together corn bread dressing because, at least in my memory, we were always able to somehow have a chicken or a turkey on those two days. It was a big deal for my four sisters, my brother, my mother and myself. I'd make a giblet gravy, get green beans ready, boil the potatoes and mash them. I always felt good when I set that spread out in front of the family.

I cook a bit now when we have time. Ellen and I like to entertain small dinner parties at home when we can. Music and cooking are two things from my growing up days that have always been a pleasure. Some of the recipes I used then stayed with me and the end products still taste good to me—and to others.

In a kitchen I was fine but as far as the rest of life went, I had no illusions. I never forgot that I couldn't read well—getting sent home from school stayed with me—so I had no great design to be a senator or a college professor. Life was a day to day process for the family and for me. I didn't like the way it was. I resented white people and the way they treated us, but I figured there was no way to fight it. I wasn't going to get up on a box in the park and shout, "You white people are being inhumane to humans."

When we were in MacGregor, Texas I can remember solving a long division problem in the fifth grade. The teacher must have been amazed that I came up with the right answer because she stood me up in front of the entire class and called me a cheater. I hadn't cheated but she sure cheated me out of some good, positive feelings about myself. I think from that time on I worked harder at sports. Sports became my way of expression. They allowed me to release my negative feelings about the world around me. Sports diminished the frustration and rejection. When I played, I wasn't shy. It was something I loved and did well.

However, life seemed to get tougher and tougher for us. In Mac-Gregor my Mom and Dad separated between my ninth and tenth birthdays. There wasn't any great explosion. He was just gone. It was like somebody holding your hand and suddenly letting go and you can never reach that hand again. We were on our own and I was now the man of the family. It didn't seem fair to me, but our lives had nothing much that was fair. I thought that was the way life was. It was a long, long time before I could understand the factors that made my father leave.

One day without any discussion, as far as I can remember, my Mom put us five kids on a train with her. She told us that we were going to San Francisco to start a new life. How right she was. San Francisco will always have a big place in my heart. The woes of Texas seemed to fall away. We were just as poor as we had been and my Mom had to scratch and scrape harder than ever. In school my reading and math abilities were still a long, long way from first team caliber, but from the first day in the school room I knew we were in a different world. It seemed to be a world where everybody got a chance. There were Mexicans, Chinese, Blacks, Irish—imagine—in the same school! In the same room! When you got on the bus you sat wherever you wanted.

There was no sign for a colored section in the movie theater. You could drink from any water bubbler you saw. I learned that whites could be nice people too, and I began to go forward again.

Sports had always attracted me. They started to stick in my system back in Texas. As I said, playing sports was the one part of my life where I could feel fully free. The first game I went for was tennis in the third grade. But tennis couldn't be a black kids' game then. It was too expensive and who was going to let you use their court? So, I started with softball. Then football. We always played football at lunch time, using a ball that the girls used playing jacks. When we were living in MacGregor the girls played basketball, so I was a little suspicious of it. It was in San Francisco that my enthusiasm for sports really started to flow. There were places to play and you could play with anybody—any color.

Right about that time of my life I discovered heroes. They were two black men who became symbols of hope for me, reasons to believe that sports could conquer color. My heroes were Joe Louis, the heavyweight champion, and Jesse Owens, the great Olympic gold medalist. Then later, of course, there was Jackie Robinson. I think every black person in the country held his breath hoping that Jackie would succeed. Yet, the idea of playing professional sports never crossed my mind. I think I idealized those black athletes because they received respect from people of all color. I wasn't able to get respect in the classroom, but I guess I hoped I could get it playing sports.

My first serious shot at a hoop was with a soccer ball in the eighth grade in a playground near where we lived in San Francisco. I wouldn't say I was good at it right away, but I was coordinated for it. I started playing everyday at a recreation center near our house or I hiked up and down the steep hills of the city for half court games of three-on-three. Wherever the action was, I went. By the time I got into Commerce High School in San Francisco, all that hustling up and down the hills of that beautiful city began to pay off. I was only 5'9" but I had developed a really deadly set shot. I broke the Triple A Prep League scoring record. I learned to become a real bulldog on defense. I always wanted to play against the other team's best man. One year in our big game against our cross town rival, Gallileo, the newspapers played up the match as a battle between K.C. Jones and Gallileo's 6'6" superstar, Don Bragg. When we played the game Bragg didn't guard me and I didn't like that: no respect. The final score was twenty-six to twenty-three. We won and I scored eighteen points.

I still wasn't a high scorer in the classroom, however. My studies were coming in third behind basketball and part-time jobs to help support the family. There was a big dip between my successes in sports and the classroom. Sometimes I just couldn't grab hold of what was being taught. I cared about school. I wanted to do well. I worked at my homework but my study habits weren't good. The world of books was still a foreign world in our house. My mother had never finished high school. It looked to me as if the best thing that could happen to K.C. Jones, the hot shot athlete of Commerce High, was to get a job carrying the mail for the US Post Office. College was only fifteen minutes away from where I lived, but I honestly didn't even know it existed. I never thought about it. There was a ceiling where I came from and you just didn't bother or even expect to go up into the attic. It was: this is me, this is where I am and this is where I'll stay.

Then something wonderful happened my senior year, and I can't call it fate. I'll call it by its real name—Miss Mildred Smith, my history teacher. Miss Smith was a white lady who saw something in this black boy that caused her to pick up the telephone and call Phil Woolpert, the basketball coach at the University of San Francisco. She didn't give up, she made more than one phone call. She kept after him to give me a scholarship to USF. She did it because she cared. Her caring changed my life. I had been selected for the All Northern California All Star Basketball team and the football team. That hadn't impressed many people, however, since nobody from any college had contacted me. Despite Mildred Smith's calls, Woolpert didn't budge until Al Corona, a sportswriter for the San Francisco *Chronicle*, came by the school and asked me what colleges were giving me a rush. I told him that nobody was. He stared at me for a minute and then grinned and said, "O.K., read my story tomorrow." The next day I read that I was being recruited by UCLA, USC, Stanford, Washington, Oregon, University of California—you name it. If I had known they existed, I would have liked Al Corona to have added Harvard and Yale. A few days later Coach Woolpert offered me the scholarship that cost the post office a great mail carrier.

I suppose I shouldn't tell this story on myself, but the day that I was to go and take the entrance exam at the University of San Francisco, I wandered all over town trying to find the place. I didn't dare let on to anybody that I didn't know where it was. I never did find the school that day. The next morning Coach Woolpert sent somebody to our door to find out what had happened to me. They brought me up to the college, which was only about fifteen minutes from our house. I held my breath and somehow passed the entrance test to USF.

During the summer between high school and college I worked in a job that left a very strong impression on me. I went down to the Union

Hiring Hall near the docks. I hung around there early every morning. After a few days, my face became familiar, I understood the system and got into it. The men would line up and be handed a colored card—either green or red or white. Those who were handed a green card were the old timers and the well connected. They got first shot at any jobs that came in. The red cards got the second chance. The white cards got whatever was left. One day an announcement came that there were six openings for a particular job at the Hide House, which didn't make any impression on me at the time. No one holding a card volunteered. Since I didn't yet have a card—you had to work first—I leaped at the chance and was assigned. I took the bus down near North Beach and as the bus went out Jackson Street I watched the numbers until we came to the end of the line. I got off and started walking. The closer I got to the number the more my nose told me what the Hide House was all about.

My job consisted of slinging and wrestling and packing wet and salted animal skins—fresh hides. At the end of the day I walked back down to the first bus stop and got on the empty bus. Perhaps out of habit from my Texas days, I sat in the back of the bus. As the bus worked its way from stop to stop into downtown San Francisco, it slowly and steadily filled with passengers. No one stayed in the back of the bus, however. By the time we got into the heart of town, the bus was jammed with people—all standing in front. I was all alone in the back of the bus, and for once I was quite sure it had nothing to do with my color. When I got home my Mom held her nose, told me to get out of my clothes at once and get in the tub.

I spent all that summer working at the Hide House. When the time came to give my notice they asked me not to leave and I was offered a full-time job packing those skins. College seemed like a wonderfully refreshing contrast as I walked down the street after my last day of work at the Hide House.

K.C. and Red Auerbach celebrate K.C.'s 200th NBA coaching victory.

K.C. drives on Wilt Chamberlain in Boston Garden.

Celtics Pride means being as proud of the team as you are of yourself.

K.C.'s goal in 1986-87 is to do a better all-around coaching job while not taking away from the players' creativity.

Bill Russell guards Jerry Lucas as K.C. Jones guards Adrian Smith.

K.C. Jones about to accept a pass from John Havlicek.

K.C. discusses a fine point of the game with a referee.

It is not an easy game.

Chapter Five

A strange thing happened to me during my summer before college. I grew four inches—which is every basketball player's dream—and I completely lost my shot—which is every basketball player's nightmare. To this day I can't understand what happened. I went from being high scorer in the city league, one of the high scorers in Northern California to an All American brick thrower. Clang—off the rim. Whew—over the backboard. Ouch—Airball! I tried everything to get my shot back. Nothing seemed to work. I made every adjustment I could think of. I didn't know it then but I would never shine on offense again. My game was forever changed and so was my life. It all began that fall at the University of San Francisco.

One man began that change; without his impact on me this book would have no reason to be written. If you're black and started in the Jim Crow South and lived on welfare with no dad around, you'll understand that I was coiled as tight as a spring when I started at USF. There was a frightening feeling of unreality as I walked around that campus. I mean, what was I doing there? I was awful lonesome. I felt the glances and heard the racial wisecracks, and it didn't exactly boost my confidence level, but it surely fueled my determination to succeed.

Phil Woolpert made all the difference. The Jesuits were firm and fair. They reached out to me, but it was Phil who put his arm around me. From the first I knew he was color blind—when you're black, you can tell. My antenna were really working in those days. With Phil we were the same, all of us on the team. He was for us—black or white. It was the beginning of the great good luck I had as a player. It began with Phil Woolpert and ended with Red Auerbach—two of the classiest men that ever walked on this earth. I know Phil once said that my getting a diploma at USF was one of the most satisfying things that ever happened to him because he knew how hard I worked for it. Phil, if it weren't for you there wouldn't have been any diploma because I wouldn't have had the courage to stay without you there.

As a freshman I started at USF and our team went seven and fourteen. I took plenty of shots as I struggled to discover what had happened to my accuracy, but I ended with a 5.6 scoring average. When the season ended, I sat down and had a long talk with myself. I had to become a different player. I would have to accept my new limits as a shooter and change my game. I decided that I would be the director—the play maker. The team would be the talent. From now on the points I would score wouldn't show up in the box score under my name, but my teammates would score more and play better because of my efforts on the floor. Parts of the game that some more talented players paid less attention to—defense and passing—I would master. I knew I could do that and I believed that if I worked as hard as possible I could still contribute an essential ingredient that the team could use. There was another factor that I knew should be the foundation for all winning teams, and in this I promised myself I would never fail. I would hustle and scrap every minute that I was on the floor in a basketball game. Nobody would ever out-hustle me. Not for one minute or part of a minute.

There were other things going on during my freshman year that were more important than my basketball problems. Sports was the world where I felt most comfortable, but the other world, the real world, outside of college and sports—the world where my mother and brother and sisters were trying to survive was occupying more and more of my thoughts and my concern. When we arrived on the West Coast from Texas we moved into a public housing project in an area that is now the Candlestick Park Football and Baseball Stadium. When I grew up there it was known as Double Rock. The project consisted of two-story, wood-framed barracks that had been built originally for people who worked building the ships at Hunter's Point during the war. The walls were made of two sheets of a kind of heavy cardboard that enclosed an inner-wall of plaster or cement. The cardboard was easily peeled off by the many restless kids who lived in Double Rock. There were no jobs way out there, and to get to downtown San Francisco to look for work was a six or seven block walk over to Third Street to catch a bus. We were on welfare from the day we arrived in the Bay area. My mom had the five of us to watch over, to feed and clothe. Although she had very little education herself, she let us know, in her quiet way, that she wanted us to get the education she had never had. By the end of my freshman year, however, I had the strong feeling that something was seriously out of kilter.

I had left the Double Rock project and lived in the dormitory at USF. I spent the year working as hard as I could at my studies and giving it all I had on the basketball court. I felt that I could succeed, that I could make it in college, but knowing the struggle my family was going through made me wonder what the point of it was. My view from the hill at USF out towards Double Rock told me that my life was a cakewalk compared to my mom's. Being born black is the quickest way to learn that life is not fair. I knew it was time for me to do something to bring some fairness to my mom's life. I was the oldest in the family, the man of the family. I had to start helping take care of the family. I decided to quit school and get a job.

Like most of the things in my life in those days, I kept all this to myself. Finally, just before the end of the school year I decided to tell Coach Woolpert that I wouldn't be back. He was really upset and told me that it would be a big mistake to pass up the opportunity of college, that the brass ring wouldn't come by again. When he asked me if my mother agreed with my decision, I told him I hadn't told my mother yet. He said he wanted to talk with my mom. He felt some other things could be done. The outcome of all this was that Coach Woolpert got my mom a job as a chambermaid at the Saint Francis Hotel, I promised my mother I'd finish college and the Jones family was off welfare.

In the fall of my sophomore year something happened that was to become a real directional arrow in my life, yet, like most of those things, I didn't know it at the time. A tall, rangy freshman walked into my room at USF and announced he was my roommate. He was tall, all right—6'9"—but other than the height difference I soon learned there were many similarities in our lives. He was black and his family had left the South for the Bay area. He was almost as cautious and watchful and quiet as I was. He was just as shy as I was. His name was Bill Felton Russell.

My association with Bill Russell has been one of the most meaningful events in my life. However, this was not apparent in the beginning. Bill says that for the first month we lived together I did not speak a single word. He says I'd slap his bunk on my way out of the room in the morning and although we ate every meal together in the cafeteria, my only contribution was to nod at the salt or sugar as we sat and ate in silence. I'm afraid Russ's memory is accurate. I was painfully shy. That was a part of my personality that made me squirm inwardly in frustration, but I didn't seem to be able to do anything about it. In high school I was really smitten by a girl. I thought she was wonderful. It was a treat for me to be near her but I never once opened my mouth. So right now, Sammy Rae Jackson, I'd like to tell you that I thought you were terrific back there in those long gone days in San Francisco. You probably thought I was practicing for the track team because every time you were nice enough to say, "Hi, K.C." I ran off like a scared jack rabbit.

That's the way things were for me in the social world. I remember getting up enough nerve to ask a girl at USF to go out on a date. This was going to be my first date and after she said yes, I didn't know what to do. All the next day I was kicking myself wishing I hadn't asked her. I didn't know what to do or where to go to duck the thing that I dreaded—talking. I was afraid to talk to people. I guess I figured I would say the wrong thing or wasn't smart enough. I know it's called shyness and that's what I was—shy—and I supose it has a cause. However, I knew one place to take the young lady where I wouldn't have to talk—we went to the movies.

Anyway, one day I started to talk to Russ and in some ways I have never stopped. He and I became inseparable. We talked of everything, of the school and the people in the school. Russell knew everyone, who all the players were and what roles they were playing on the campus. He would analyze everybody from the president, to our coach, to the janitors. We talked about life, of being black in a white society. He and I spent long hours discussing people's attitudes toward us as black student-athletes. We often heard those sly remarks made by some of the white students. I guess we weren't supposed to be smart enough to understand remarks that were degrading to us. Russ and I would talk about the why's of those attitudes. But most of all we talked about basketball.

Sitting here now trying to find the proper words to explain the conversations that Bill Russell and I had about basketball is very difficult. I find it curious that I can't easily explain those conversations because they were easy and they were endless. Somehow we both realized that basketball was a game of vertical and horizontal angles. The more we talked, the more this fascinated us. We invented our own court language to describe plays, moves, counter-moves and strategies. In attempting to be precise in putting all this into understandable language, I realize the printed word isn't able to catch the magic of those conversations. It was like two minds working in the same direction with the same thoughts and the same goals. Often we finished one another's sentences and thoughts.

Of course there was more than conversation between Russ and myself. In practice we'd battle each other as though we were biting enemies. We were always trying to determine ways to make the opponent take the shot that we wanted him to take from the place where we wanted him to try and shoot. I guess by the time we graduated from USF Bill Russell and I had talked, studied, worked, practiced and played as much defensive basketball as any two people ever had.

While all this was going on, something else was happening with the USF basketball program. We had a squad of about seventeen players and I guess we were what you would call underachievers. We had some nice talent, a number of players who could do everything you wanted to be able to do on the basketball court. But the team didn't win. Some of those talented players felt they were above their teammates, and this superior attitude kept us from being a team because a team is a group of players who support one another on the court and who think of the group before they think of themselves. So my sophomore year was a repeat of my freshman year at USF, but I figured the big freshman sitting on the bench would help change things around for us in my junior year.

I suspect we all learn as we work our way through life that the things that we take for granted can sometimes disappear in a moment. That almost happened to me in my junior year. We opened with an upset win at the University of California. After the game I felt the kind of pain that I had had once during my senior year of high school. I spent two weeks in bed then, in real pain, unable to eat, almost unable to move. We had no doctor to call, no money to pay for a hospital, so I lay in bed and got through it. Now, I felt that same pain again. The next day the team was on a bus bound for a game at Fresno and my stomach was doing flips. When the bus pulled into town, its first stop was the hospital. The doctors found that the pain was caused by a burst appendix, and they couldn't figure out why I hadn't had serious problems earlier. My appendix was too enlarged to operate. Of course, I learned all this after the fact, because by the time they got me off the team bus I was in agony and I stayed unconscious for four days. I was hanging onto life by my fingernails. When my condition was at its worst, the University of San Francisco student body was asked to turn out for a special service to pray for my recovery. Hundreds of kids showed up. It was an event that really touched Bill Russell—although not quite enough, since he didn't remember to tell me about it until about two years after it happened.

A week after I was admitted to the hospital, I had some idea of where I was and what was happening. I was also twenty-five pounds lighter and too weak to get out of bed. I was truly lucky to be alive. There was no question about making a decision—the season was over for me. I sat on the bench and watched Russell and my teammates build a fourteen and seven season, and Russ and I continued our never ending analysis of the game of basketball.

Something else happened to me at the University of San Francisco that was very important in my life. I became intrigued with the possibility of becoming an educated man. I truly enjoyed school, and didn't miss more than three or four days during my college career. I would be misleading the reader and would probably give my old coach Phil Woolpert and some of my teachers a good belly laugh if I implied that I was a wizard with the books. I wasn't, and I think the coach kept his fingers crossed that I would remain eligible. I needed tutoring and had to work very hard. Things that took other people ten minutes to read seemed to take me a half an hour. Yet I enjoyed learning. I wanted a college education and I was proud of the fact that I was getting one. My mother and my brother and sisters and I had expended most of our energies just surviving. Now, not having to worry about a roof over my head, getting three square meals and having this opportunity to learn was very exciting. I didn't want to miss any of it. Even though I had to struggle, the rewards were worth it.

I was fascinated with courses like epistemology and ontology and psychology. My Jesuit teachers didn't rush me. They seemed to understand that I was proud of what I was doing and wanted to understand as much as possible. I learned that the basis of all philosophy was common sense. This thought has stayed with me. I try to keep it in mind in all the circumstances that I encounter. I learned long ago that I could learn by talking less and listening more. When the talking and the listening are done, I try to reach a common sense answer. Sports and studies in college gave me a sense of confidence in my own instincts, and I know when I stick with a common sense answer I have the best chance of succeeding.

B ill Russell wasn't the only super athlete at the University of San Francisco in those days. We had a football team that made all the pro scouts' mouths water. People like Ollie Matson, Burl Tolar, and Ed Brown. Those guys were about as tough as tough can be. Most of that team grew up in San Francisco. I remember as a kid watching them scrimmage —playing tackle football with no pads, no equipment of any kind, banging away at one another on a hard gravel surface. Maybe it was when I was watching those tigers tear into one another that I decided that I loved basketball.

In the fall of my freshman year those fellows had an awesome team. They crushed every team they played and went through the entire season undefeated. As I was walking to class one day with the great Ollie Matson, he said to me, "Well, we've done it, now you guys go ahead and do it."

I looked at him and said, "What do you mean?"

He said, "Go undefeated. The football team was undefeated. Now let's have that basketball team go undefeated."

I don't remember what my response was. Probably a grunt. But I do remember thinking, "Is he serious? The basketball team go undefeated?"

Ollie Matson was a wise man. Or a prophet.

I had two more years of basketball eligibility because of my illness. Those two years brought results for our team that were beyond anything I had ever dreamed of. Our record was fifty seven and one. We set an NCAA record of winning fifty-six straight games and won back-to-back national titles.

I think the drive and energy that characterized those two wonderful years were ignited by something that happened at the beginning of our first record setting seasons. We were invited to play in a tournament in Oklahoma City. There were eight teams in the tournament. We were seeded 8th—if you can call that a seed. On our way to Oklahoma City, we learned that we were ranked to finish 500th that year in college basketball in the United States. Obviously, the other seven teams in the tournament were not staying awake worrying about playing us.

The arrangement for practicing for this tournament was an unusual one. The court was somewhat like a stage with the seats lower than the playing surface. Spectators wandering in to watch practice looked up at us. As I recall our squad of seventeen had only four or five whites. As we practiced, the spectators' comments and wisecracks became more and more racist. About the nicest thing they called us were "Globetrotters." They punctuated nasty remarks by throwing pennies, nickles and maybe even a few dimes up on the stage. In the middle of this Russell stopped practice, got down and scooped up the money from the floor and carried it over to the coach saying in a loud voice, "Save this money for us, Coach, and we'll spend it on a victory party."

The fact that the "fans" there considered us some kind of circus attraction created tremendous anger and frustration in us, and we talked about it that day after practice. Their attitude caused us to play even tougher basketball. We hustled more than ever in that tournament. It triggered feelings in us that made us more intense and even grouchier in our games. We won our way to the finals and played the University of Oklahoma team that was rated as one of the top teams in the country. We destroyed them. Late in the game, standing at the foul line, one of their players turned to me and said with real honest to goodness admiration in his voice, "You guys are really terrific. What a great team you've got."

I've never forgotten that. I thought it was such a compliment and it said it all. We had become a great team. That tournament was the beginning of two wonderful years that taught me important lessons about team play, about the necessity of supporting your teammates, that I have never forgotten. These same concepts or attutudes—to an even greater degree—have been the heart of our great Celtics teams.

Our championship teams at USF did not have a single player who was a pure, high-scoring shooter. Our victories had to be achieved with everyone contributing. Bill Russell, of course, with his intense defensive play, his shot blocking and rebounding was the heart and soul of the team, but never once in those years did he ever indicate that he thought he was above the team. Russ had struggled in high school as a basketball player. He sat on the bench for three years and only got to play in his senior year. He received his scholarship to USF primarily because of the efforts of Hal DeJulio, a USF graduate who sensed Bill would be an asset to the team, not because he was a highly talented high school star. Yet without being known as a great basketball player or looking like an movie idol, Russ somehow managed to sustain a self-confidence and an ego that were bigger than all of us. It was strange but we were all better because of his confidence. We fed on it and increased our own sense of self.

Strange that after all these years I've found another person who has the same intense certainty and the impressive skill to support it that Russ had. In 1980 Bill was voted the greatest player in the history of the NBA. Larry Bird may match that honor one day. Talk about being in the right place at the right time!

At USF, just like in Boston, we were quick to pat a teammate on the butt when he made a mistake to let him know mistakes were another thing we had in common. We never criticised one another's play. Our goal was the team's success. Everyone on the squad, black and white, believed the team came first. Our coach, Phil Woolpert, made every one of us feel valuable and important to the team. He gave us a pattern to follow and let us use our skills to modify or change that pattern as we needed to; and that told us he believed in us. All these combined factors created a championship basketball team that seized and held the whole country's attention.

The attitude that we had at USF is the same philosophy that Red Auerbach instilled in us with the Celtics. Phil Woolpert and Red were alike in another way too. Tough as they might be, they like to have a team that can laugh and have fun. I can't say I learned that from them because that's my style too. They did teach me that in coaching, fun and relaxation combined with disciplined hard work, add up to better results than all the X's and O's ever scratched on a blackboard. My years as a Celtics player gave me plenty of reasons for chuckles, and that fit in with what I had learned at USF. Lots of very hard work and practice produce the rewards of winning and laughing.

In the pros, of course, there is always the added attraction of extra money. At USF our bonus was a trip to South America. It's another one of my happy memories and like so many of them, it comes from playing basketball. After we won our first NCAA championship, our faculty advisor, Father Tichner, held a meeting and told us that the college had accepted an invitation to tour some of the big cities in South America and play exhibition basketball games. He said that since USF was a Jesuit school, the entire South America college network was waiting for us with open arms. He warned us that we should be on our best behavior, that we would be guests in these countries and that the first thing we should realize is that it is rude to be late. He warned us that the people of South America are punctual and he expected all of us to be on time for every event. He also mentioned being careful of drinking water and eating certain foods.

Our trip was a great experience. Parts of South America shocked me. Lord knows I had lived through some tough patches growing up, but I had never seen anything like some of the living conditions that we saw in South America. It made me aware that both deprivation and gain are relative.

Father Tichner somehow managed to be late for most of the events on the trip. These included airplane, bus and train departures. He would come puffing up at the last minute only to have one of the wise guys on the team threaten to shut the door in his face because he was not being prompt. One of my teammates, Bill Bush, talked one of the airlines into a funny prank one day and we rolled down the runway roaring with laughter while tardy Father Tichner screamed and waved at us to come back. When we went back to get him, his excuse was—as always—that the South Americans he was dealing with were never on time.

I remember an occasion when our plane arrived late for a game scheduled in a soccer stadium in the mountains of Bolivia. We rushed from the plane to the airport and then to the stadium. When we got to the stadium, we were too exhausted to do anything but sit and breathe deeply. The altitude had done us in. We couldn't have gotten the ball up to the hoop. There was no game.

The water and the food or the combination did get to us all from time to time. We took turns having upset stomachs and worse. This created a funny moment in Lima, Peru where we were scheduled to play a game in the bullring at the local stadium. We drew big crowds for games all over South America. They seemed to like basketball and that day the bullring was jammed. Three or four of the guys were sick. They tried to warm up but told coach they just couldn't play. Just as the game was about to begin, Coach Woolpert pointed at a kid named Lopez who was on the squad but seldom played and told him to take off his warm-ups—he was going to start in the game. Lopez bent over and pulled off his warm-up pants and he and the crowd and Father Tichner, who was arriving late for the game, all discovered simultaneously that Lopez had no shorts on—just a jockstrap. He presented a San Francisco moon for the South American crowd and the Peruvian fans roared with laughter. It was that kind of memory that we cherished as a group. It made individuals a more closely knit team.

Thirty years later it's that same sense of togetherness and comradeship that I am trying to maintain with this 1985–1986 Celtics team, although I don't plan to ask anyone to repeat the Lopez, South American, bullring performance at the Boston Garden.

Chapter Six

Some of the best coaches in the game believe that basketball is primarily a game of one-on-one. The offensive player has the ball and his object is to score, to beat his man and put the ball in the hoop. The defensive player's job is to prevent the man with the ball from scoring. This certainly is a key ingredient to the game.

For me, however, a basketball team at its best is like a great musical group. Each member must contribute what is required at the precise moment and yet, like a great jazz band, there must be respect and confidence in the exceptional talents to allow them spontaneous execution. Harmony is essential in the making of a winning team. Being good at playing one-on-one basketball is not enough. There must be the team-feeling. Players who have exceptional talent but do not want to give their all for the team are better off elsewhere. A winning team has no place for stars who think they shine brighter than the rest of the team.

I don't know if I can define what the sportswriters call Celtics Pride. One of the things I can say is that Celtics Pride means to be as proud of the team as you are of yourself—to know that the team's success is your success. I've never seen a better example of two stars giving themselves to team harmony and success than I've seen on this year's Celtics team. Robert Parish and Bill Walton are the two stars. They are stars both on and off the court and they proved it this season.

Bill Walton came to the team as a basketball legend. He had won National Championships in college where he broke our USF record.

He had been the key factor in leading Portland to a big win in the NBA in 1978. It seemed he had done everything there is to do in basketball. He is no kid. In fact, Larry Bird loves to razz him by telling him that when Larry and his pals were little and playing in the backyards of French Lick, Indiana, Bill was their hero.

Walton wanted to play winning basketball again. He wanted to be a Celtic. He wanted to be a Celtic so much that he gave up quite a sum to leave the Los Angles Clippers and come to Boston. Bill Walton is a great center. He tells everybody that he's 6'11." Robert Parish has been our star center for some years. Robert is about a half inch over seven feet, and Bill Walton is a good inch taller than Robert Parish. I'm sure there isn't a coach alive who wouldn't like to have both players on their team. Yet, my first reaction to Walton coming was, "Great, but . . ." I knew that if Walton and Parish didn't get along, if there was any resentment on the part of either one, Bill Walton's coming to the Celtics could be a negative. Because of the series of serious, damaging injuries that Bill has suffered over the last several years, Bill's playing time had been restricted. Yet, I knew he wasn't coming to Boston to play four or five minutes and then sit on the bench. I was sure he felt that he was ready to play a lot of intense basketball again. That, of course, could help our team. One of the problems we had last year was that I had to play Robert so many minutes that he was running out of gas by the end of the season. A Walton could change all that, but only if he understood that Robert was our starting center and that he was a backup.

It was vital that Parish see Walton's arrival not as a threat to his role on the club, but as a large helping hand toward the team's success. That is exactly what happened. Bill Walton, wisely, called Robert Parish before the trade was made. They talked at length about their feelings of playing time and personal and team goals. This was a good beginning, and as the year went on their relationship seemed to get better and better. They obviously enjoy practicing hard against one another. They enjoy one another's success during games. We've done some things socially with the two of them and their wives and children to foster that Celtics family feeling. The fact is that any time I spent worrying about the Parish/Walton/Celtics relationship was wasted time.

Robert Parish is a big man in every sense of the word. He is a different man than the fans see. He is a witty, compassionate guy. He was not in the slightest bit threatened by Bill Walton's arrival. He understood that with the addition of Bill the team would be stronger and Robert's career might well be longer. There is almost a little bit of poetry in those lines and that's precisely the way having Bill Walton and Robert Parish on the same team worked out—as smooth as poetry. They are both complete professionals. They are both outstanding human beings.

Bill Walton's intensity and desire to win has made this a better year for all of us. Like Larry Bird, he is obsessed with winning basketball and perfection. On a Southwest road trip during the year, I was walking behind a group of Celtics who were crossing the street in front of the hotel. It was around noon and we were playing at eight o'clock that night. The players were kidding one another, laughing, and very relaxed. Suddenly, I heard Bill say to them, "Come on you guys, we've gotta start getting serious. We gotta start thinking about the game tonight." He was more serious than he was joking. He has earned the respect of everyone on the team. Early in the season he was having his problems handling the ball and even with his passing and he is probably the greatest passing center of all time. I took him aside and told him that I thought he was putting too much pressure on himself by trying to do too much. I said that perhaps because he had had to carry other teams he'd played with, he felt the same responsibility here. I told him that he didn't need to do it all with the Celtics, that other people would help him carry the weight here. From that point on he seemed to go with the flow of the team more and more.

As this season progressed Bill created something that is becoming a tradition for us. Before our games, we have something of a pregame scenario: Jimmy Rodgers will go over the defensive moves that we hope to make; I will talk a little bit about offense or overall strategy for the night and ask if there are any questions or comments—I always want to get the players input. There is usually a brief quiet moment after that and then we head out of the locker room. Sometime early in the season during that quiet moment before going out onto the court, Bill Walton stood up and in a very intense voice said, "O.K. let's go out and get those suckers." We're all pros, but I think that moment put an extra charge of electricity in all of us. Now before every game without a word being spoken we all wait for Bill to stand up and say the magic words.

Chapter Seven

Strange the way things work in life. After being concerned about team harmony and media flack when I cut David Thirdkill, that wheel has turned full circle. Thirdkill is back with the team because Sly Williams is gone. Just like that—Sly Williams disappeared.

When we brought Sly here from Atlanta he was a player tagged with being difficult on and off the court. The Celtics have taken players like that over the years and turned them around. Our approach to the game and the concept of the team as a family usually work to bring out the best in a player. I thought this was working with Sly. In our first conversation I told him that he couldn't expect big minutes but that I thought he could look to ten, twelve, fifteen minutes of playing time. I should have said ten, twelve, fifteen or zero because he didn't get in some of the early games. Then he had some injury problems that needed to be corrected. We were at Logan getting ready for a road trip and I noticed that he seemed very uncomfortable. When I asked him if he was alright, he said he had a very bad toothache. I had trainer Ray Melchiorre take a look at him. Since neither Ray nor I have x-ray vision, we decided Sly ought to get himself to a dentist. We left him behind and went off on our road trip. Three or four days passed and nobody heard from Sly. Finally I called his wife about six o'clock one night and asked to speak with him. His wife told me that he was in Hartford seeing a doctor. Whatever happened, we may never know, but we never heard from Sly again. We looked at players available around the country and we decided to bring David Thirdkill back from

Portland, Maine where he had been playing in the minor leagues.

I think this is the proper time to confess that I was once guilty of disappearing from a professional sports organization. In my case it was the Los Angeles Rams football team.

I was drafted by the Boston Celtics in the second round of the pro-basketball draft in 1956. My best pal, Bill Russell, had been drafted by the Celtics in the first round. I guess by that time Russell and Jones had become household words as far as college basketball went. The idea of playing with Bill on the Celtics was very exciting. Certainly, playing pro basketball was in my mind. The great George Mikan – of what used to be the Minneapolis Lakers – talked to me about quitting college in my senior year and playing for the Lakers. He offered me a five thousand dollar bonus, which seemed like all the money in the US Treasury, but I knew my mom wanted me to get an education and my degree. I pictured myself handing that money to my mom but I knew in my heart that she'd be much more pleased seeing me with that diploma in my fist. I sure was tempted by the idea of getting paid for playing basketball. But I had some common sense from my philosophy courses that, I suppose, brought me a touch of fear that I might fail. Let's face it – I was 6'1" and I couldn't shoot the ball. I figured there were probably about twelve million other guys the Celtics could have drafted with the same qualities. I made a decision that many people thought was a little goofy at the time, but as I look back on it, what I did made it possible for me to play with the Celtics later on. I joined the Army.

They were still drafting in those days. It was fair then – everybody was supposed to serve. I figured I might as well get it over with, so I went down to Union Square and volunteered for the Army. Even though my service time was all peacetime and mostly enjoyable, I'm glad now that I'm a veteran. At one stage of my Army career I was stationed at Fort Leonard Wood in Missouri. I soldiered as a company clerk typist and also spent time working in the regimental post office. While I was there I played wide receiver on the football team. One of my teammates was John Morrow, who had played center for the Los Angeles Rams. Morrow told me that he believed I had a career as a pro-football player. He called the Rams and talked to them about me. The world being the small place that it is, the man Morrow talked to was Pete Rozelle who was then general manager of the Rams and is now Commissioner of the National Football League. Before reaching those summits in his career he had been Director of Public Relations at the University of San Francisco. He had already tried to interest me in pro football when I was a freshman at USF and he knew he was headed for the general manager position with the Rams. Rozelle knew me and knew what I could do and thought Morrow's idea was a good one. The Rams wrote and invited me to their training camp.

When I arrived at the Rams training camp I weighed 195 pounds and I was in good shape. Sid Gilman was the coach of the Rams and he started me off as a receiver. I got off to a kind of wobbly start, maybe because I didn't run the pass routes quite right or I got there too fast. Whatever it was, he switched me to defensive back and immediately I knew I had found a home. If I sound like I'm bragging it's because I am when I tell you that nobody completed any passes around me. I started as a defensive back in the Rams first three exhibition games. After the third game, however, I developed a nasty muscle tear in my thigh which somehow or other grew into a pretty good sized lump. It was as hard as a brick. I was told that this was a calcium deposit. It was giving me a lot of discomfort and I felt the situation needed a couple of days of rest. I went to practice that day without pads. When the coach asked me why, I said my leg needed a little time out. He said the trainers had told him the leg wouldn't be damaged if I scrimmaged and played the following Sunday. He told me to get my pads. I did that—he was the coach and I scrimmaged. But that night I made a decision about my so-called football career.

I called Red Auerbach to see if there was a life for me in basketball. Red invited me to the Celtics camp which would start in three weeks. I went to Sid Gilman and told him that I was thinking about trying the Celtics. He asked me not to leave and said I was going to be a hell of a defensive back. I thought it all out. The next day, without a word to anybody, I packed my bag and left the Rams camp. I never did explain myself to Pete Rozelle. I feel badly about that. So now, after all these years, Pete, I'd like to apologize for not having called or written. I suppose it's too late to tell you that I've decided to try and make a career out of basketball.

As I look back on my life it seems to me that the events I thought were setbacks or detours have actually been or developed into turns that somehow brought me up in front of opportunity. It happened with the appendix problem in college when I had to miss a semester of school and not play for a season. That caused Russell and me to play our junior and senior years together and having those two great years as the best team in college basketball. I know it's fair to say that if I hadn't played on those USF teams with Russell, no one would have noticed me and I wouldn't have been drafted by the Celtics. Added to that is my strong belief that if I had gone to a tryout with the Celtics straight from college, I would not have made the squad.

The time I spent in the Army gave me an opportunity that I had never dreamed would come my way—the sweet experience of playing basketball for the United States Olympic Team. In 1952, when I was a freshman at USF, a fellow named Hal DeGulio who had played on the USF NIT team of 1949 was working out with us. One day after practice he said, "You know, this is an Olympic year. Some of you guys could get invited to go to the Olympics. If not this time, next time. You might go then, K.C."

I remember thinking to myself that this man couldn't be serious. Representing our country in the Olympics was not the kind of thing that was going to happen to a nobody from San Francisco. I suppose if I really scratch my memory I would have to admit that I must have thought, a black welfare kid from San Francisco. But once again the unimaginable became reality. Four years later Russell and I were picked for the College All Stars and our team participated in what was called the Olympic Tournament. Once again, I'm sure my association with Russ got me noticed. We didn't win the tournament. We were beaten by the Phillips 66 Oilers, but three of us from the college team were picked for the Olympic squad. I was a little surprised that all three of us were black. Carl Cain, an all American from the University of Iowa, Russell and myself were chosen from the college team. We were the only black players on the squad. Soon after the squad was chosen I was ordered to report to the Army base at Fort Lewis, Seattle, Washington.

The Army was pleased that I was going to participate in the Olympics. They cut orders for me to report to Baltimore, Maryland where the team was beginning an exhibition tour that had us play all across the United States, in Hawaii and the Fiji Islands. In November we arrived in Melbourne, Australia where the Olympic Games were to be held.

Carl Cain became a great pal with Russell and me. Carl had the misfortune to suffer a badly injured back during an exhibition game, but the Olympic Committee was terrific in letting him stay with the squad. Carl brought a lot to the team even though he wasn't able to play. He was a truly classy guy of great intelligence and good humor. He also had a wonderful sister—someone you'll hear more of later. We had many laughs together. I remember one day when he and Russell and I made our first visit to downtown Melbourne to go to a movie. We strolled down the main street, 6'9" Russell, 6'4" Cain and myself, all very nicely tanned. Suddenly we realized that we were collecting a crowd behind us. We could hear their comments, "Africans! Africans! They must be Zulus from Africa!" The group dogging our heels got to be sixty or seventy people. Russell didn't miss a beat. He started to speak to us in a loud voice, "Uuga baga yugo gali maga." We answered, "Uga—Uga." And so it went as the crowd grew and whispered and chuckled behind us all the way to the movie theater.

Our Olympic coach was Gerald Tucker. He was a wonderful, laid-back Southwesterner who has sinced passed away. He had the coaching philosophy that I was fortunate enough to deal with during my basketball-playing days. Gerry believed strongly in the theory that the basketball team that is a happy family will probably be a winning basketball team. I believe our Olympic Team saw ourselves as a kind of American family—different races, different colors, but with the same team goals.

We opened against the Japanese. I don't think their biggest man made it to 6'4". We countered with Chuck Darling, a 7' All American center and forwards who were 6'8" and 6'10". In his pre-game talk Coach Tucker said, "We'll play them full court pressure—K.C. you're terrific at it. You did it at USF and Ford, (who's now an executive vice president with Converse Shoe Company and a great guy) I know that you'll try and do just as good a job as K.C.

The first time the Japanese team brought the ball up court, my man had the ball and I was all over him—then, zip—he went past me like a streak. This happened to us a couple of more times and coach knew it was time for a little chat. During the time out as we stood around looking at the Japanese in amazement, the coach said we better start picking them up at half court. Finally, we worked our way down to picking them up at the top of the key. After we got straightened out, we buried them. We rolled over the rest of our opposition. Our toughest game was in the finals where we beat the Russians by fourteen or fifteen points.

When the moment of awarding the Gold Medals arrived and I stood listening to the Star Spangled Banner, I thought to myself that wild things do happen—that I should have the good luck to be standing in this stadium in Australia as a representative of my country was beyond any dreams I had ever had. I remember marching around the track behind the American flag thinking of the thousands and thousands of basketball players in America and the thousands who were stars and feeling that I was the luckiest guy in the world.

Something else happened during my Olympic experience that had what some writers call a profound effect on my life. As I said earlier, after training camp the Olympic team toured the United States. One of our many stops for an exhibition game was Peoria, Illinios. Russell and Carl Cain and I were standing in the hotel lobby and a lovely young woman walked up to us and gave Carl a big hug. I was pleased when Carl told me this was his sister, Beverly. I was surprised that my pal Carl had not told me about her before. The four of us went in to dinner and Beverly and I seemed to find lots to talk about. As I remember it, Russ and Carl excused themselves right after they were finished eating. That didn't make me mad. Beverly and I talked on and on. Old closemouthed K.C. disappeared. Folks came in and had their meals and left. Other people filled their spots and Beverly and I talked on and on.

I wrote Beverly a note a couple of days after the team left Peoria. We began a correspondence that continued for the next two years.

K.C. Jones and his sister Eula Mae.

K.C. Jones played on two NCAA title teams at the University of San Francisco.

USF's team is welcomed back home after winning an NCAA crown.

University of San Francisco's NCAA championship winning team.

K.C. Jones as a player on the 1956 Olympic Gold Medal Team.

I believe our Olympic Team saw ourselves as a kind of American family—different races, different colors, but with the same team goals.

Chapter Eight

The time had come to see if I could make the grade with the Boston Celtics. Three years had passed since they had drafted me. That passage of time proved crucial to my career. My Army years made me a better, stronger player than I had been when I graduated from USF. This was a better time for me. A team loaded with great players was getting older. Despite the fact that in Bob Cousy and Bill Sharman the Celtics had the two finest guards in basketball, I made the squad. I'm sure it was by the skin of my teeth—but I made it. Years later Red said that funny things seemed to happen when he put me into a game. He said it seemed as though I wasn't doing anything that he could put his finger on, but it looked like our team always improved when I was out there. If we were behind when I walked in, we were closer when I got out. If we were ahead when I came in, we increased our lead by the time I came out. It's true I even made every practice a war. I guess I did such a job in the scrap and hustle department that they decided to keep me around.

For the first time in my life I was sitting on the bench. I learned to get used to it because I sat on the bench for the next five years. Some players can't stand this type of situation, but I believe that if the player spends as much time thinking about the team as he does about himself he will be comfortable with his job—even if that involves riding the pine and being a cheerleader because, believe me, that helps too. I instantly understood what my role was. I knew I wasn't a Cousy or a Sharman. I'd watch and not worry about being a star or a starter.

When Red pointed his finger at me to go into the ballgame, I knew he wanted ferocious defense on the other team's toughest guard, sharp, crisp passes, and all the hustle I had. I gave the team everything I had every time. I made sure I was always ready.

It's funny, I never thought about replacing either one of those great players. It was almost a day-to-day game-to-game thing with me. If I had known at that time that I would be around as long as I have, I'd have been very happy.

R ed Auerbach once said, "The Celtics aren't a team—they are a way of life."

That's a fact and I'd like to explain what that way of life was like when I had the good fortune to spend nine years with a team that won the NBA title eight consecutive years. If I can tell it like it was, perhaps it will help clarify what I try to achieve now as a coach.

It's almost impossible to describe the feeling that the players on our teams had for one another. Everybody—Satch, Russell, Havlicek, Cous, Heinie, to name a few—bring back any name that spent time with the Celtics in those years and I know they would say what I'm saying. Every player on those winning teams supported his team-mates. Most people wouldn't believe this but I remember that when Don Nelson joined the club, Satch was quick to go over to him and say, "Keep doing this on defense and concentrate on such and such a move on your rebounding and you can take my starting job."

That happened just as I'm telling it because everybody on that team pulled for every other man on the team. We understood each other. We had great personal ties on the court and off the court and pos-sessed a sense of togetherness that you could feel. I've never thought about belonging to an elite club or fraternity, but the feeling we had with the Celtics was that we belonged to the most exclusive club in the world.

With my ability it was a kind of miracle that I belonged to that club. Here was far and away the best team in basketball setting a champion-ship winning record that's never been equaled in professional sports, and I was playing on that team. I probably would have been lucky to make the bench on any other team in the league. That may sound strange, but although the Celtics were the best team in basketball they were probably the only team in the league I could have played for. That's because the Celtics were different. There was Sam the Shooter, Heinie the shooter, Satch the rebounder/defender, Cous the great passer and shooter and of course, Russ the passer and shot blocker and rebounder extrordinaire—and me, playing defense, all the time as hard as I could. We each had our job. We were part of a unit and that unit made each of us stronger. We pulled for each other and understood each other. Here we were, grown men, working at the highest level in a very competitive profession, yet, we were proud of one another. That pride in each other cranked up another notch to our pride in our team. There was a closeness and that closeness made all the difference.

Our togetherness extended way beyond the lines of the court, and it still does. We did things socially—all of us. If someone was having a party, everyone on the squad was invited—always. There were no twosomes or threesomes then, and there aren't any now. It's something I keep a close eye on as a coach. The word is cliques and I know that they can be destructive to a team. The Celtics don't have that problem. That tradition started with Red, and Russell added to it. It is certainly one of the cornerstones of Celtic pride. I remember Orlando Cepeda, the baseball player, being at a Celtics party at somebody's house and he seemed absolutely amazed by it. He stood beside me, taking in the scene, and said, "I've been playing professional baseball for twenty years and I've never seen anything like this with a baseball team. You've got everybody here. Black guys, white guys, and their wives, and you can tell you people get along. I know guys who have been on the Red Sox for years and never exchanged two words outside the ballpark and maybe just about that many at the ballpark."

My hair may be getting a touch of grey, but most other things haven't changed with the Celtics. Robert Parish's wife, Nancy, made her jazz-singing debut up in Manchester, New Hampshire, her hometown. Everybody was there. During her last number the players and coaches and Jan Volk, Celtics general manager went up on the stage and sang with her. It was a terrific moment for all of us. The event made me feel very good about our team.

The relationship between the wives and the team is something that's vital to a team's harmony. Players' wives suffer as much as the players and sometimes more. They deserve the attention and respect of coaches and management and their husbands.

We had the same kind of understanding on the court that we tried for elsewhere. For example, Tommy Heinsohn loved to shoot the ball. Now if Tommy had been with some other club, he might very well have heard some of his teammates wondering out loud about some of the shots he took. With the Celtics he took his shots with our blessing. We respected him as a competitor, a great shooter and most of all as a man, and we knew he respected us as men and as players who had our own unique contribution to make to the team. Things mattered to the Celtics that didn't matter to other teams—lots of things. Some of them might seem small or trivial to the fans or to other players, but they aren't. The examples that come to my mind are endless, but I'll only give you a couple.

The first is from the Celtics experience of the great John Havlicek. John came to us in 1962 from a great Ohio State team—and he was not the star of that team. So, here he was a rookie on a team that had won the championship six years in a row. A team led by a big, intense, black man named Bill Russell. One day after practice, soon after he arrived at camp, John mentioned that he was looking to buy a stereo and wondered where the best place would be to get one. Russell heard this and the next thing John knew he was in Russell's car being chauffeured around town in a search for the best deal available. John couldn't get over it. Here was the superstar, the man with a reputation of being touchy about the black-white thing, breaking his butt for the young rookie. This was the kind of thing that the rest of us on the team took for granted. It was Russell's way and it became the Celtics way. John Havlicek learned that day that Celtics help one another off and on the court and that every man on the team is valued as a human being.

For me a different story taught the same lesson. Despite my days at USF, the Olympics, the Army and the Rams, I was still the quiet man when my Celtics career started. Off the basketball court I had nothing to say. I simply didn't have the confidence. Although I still believe a man is better off if he does more listening than talking, you've got to be able to communicate to get along in this world. My teammates were well aware of my situation and one day they presented me with a membership in The Toastmaster's Club, an organization that teaches people to talk on their feet. Some fellows might have been offended by their effort, but I knew that it was done to help me along the way and to smooth the path that I was trying to follow. The media can get the wrong idea about someone who doesn't talk. They pass their impression on to the fans and then you've got a player whose career is in trouble. I appreciated the good thoughts behind my teammates' offer; however, I was never able to participate. Later, Dale Carnegie courses did help me gain some public-speaking skills.

I don't want you to think that I was totally tongue-tied in those days. As a matter of fact, when I was with just my teammates, I had as much fun as they did and was a very talkative guy. I became a leader in the singing sessions we'd have in the shower or in the locker room. I could imitate Red's walk and talk and I'd grab a cigar and do a little Auerbach routine that got a lot of laughs—and there were a lot of laughs with the Celtics. Nobody and nothing were sacred. Anybody who was feeling a little bit bigger than life got cut down to size in a hurry.

With this year's team it's the star of stars, Mr. L. Bird, who does the deflating better than anybody else. He is the shrewd, witty philosopher of the team. And like all good teachers, his style is catching. Kevin McHale, whose game gets better and better and, I'm especially pleased to say, gets tougher and tougher as our season moves along, continues to be the Mr. Yakkety Yak of the team. He's always good for a lengthy interview with the media, which sometimes can be like walking through a mine field, but he's damn good at it—never seems to get himself or the rest of us blown up. Some of the other players watch him in amazement. I remember after one of our games Jerry Sichting turned to some of the other players and asked if they were sure that Kevin's brain was connected to his tongue. I think the reporters who heard the remark were jolted. As the players were chuckling, I knew that crack meant that Jerry Sichting had really arrived as a Celtic. A chuckle between teammates is as good as a three point play.

With the old Celtics there was Satch, the leader of laughter. He had a way about him that brightened up the world. The two of us became really close and I think his style put some polish on me. He was a serious man who didn't take himself too seriously. He could tell a story about himself that would have the locker room roaring with laughter. And through it all, he would keep his dignity.

There are stories about Satch, the automobile owner and driver, that kept us laughing off and on for years. When Satch had safely made the team and realized that he was going to have all of seven or eight thousand bucks a year salary to spend, he decided that it was time for him to own a car. He made this announcement to us one day and at the same time admitted that he did not know how to drive. Everybody on the squad became Satch's driving teacher—for a time. Heinsohn, Russell, Ramsey, Cousy, I think we all took a turn with Satch and agreed that he was the world's slowest and most cautious driver. We had a little party and drank a few beers to celebrate when he passed his driving test—which was another great adventure I'll talk about in a bit. The next order of business was Satch buying the car. He had been checking out every automobile dealer in New England while he was doing his practice driving with us. On the day after he got his license he got behind the wheel of a new Pontiac. He was late for practice that day and Red asked him what was going on. He told us the story of his first day behind the wheel as a licensed driver.

He was driving through Cambridge in heavy traffic—trucks and buses and cars all around him. He's looking sideways, and in the rear-view mirror, checking out everybody, making sure no one would scratch or dent his shiny fenders. A huge truck was snorting and growling right behind him. Of course, Satch was traveling at his usual speed of about three miles an hour. The traffic got worse and worse, stop and go, stop and go. The horns were blowing behind him like crazy but he didn't care—he's still checking from side to side and behind him, making sure he doesn't get too close to anybody and nobody gets too close to him. In typical Satch story telling style, he was acting out the whole scenario, and the whole team was standing with their eyes glued on Satch the actor—hands on the imaginary wheel, head and eyes swiveling from side to side and up into the mirror to check the other traffic. Now he looked ahead again, still speeding along like a crab at three miles an hour. There was a cop lying on the hood of his car, waving and screaming. Satch brought the Pontiac to a tiptoe stop. Everything had come to a screeching halt. People were getting out of their cars to look at the sight. The cop lay there staring at him through the windshield. Finally he climbed down and asked to take a look at Satch's license. It turned out the cop was a Celtics fan. He saw that the ink was still wet on the license so he pushed Satch into the passengers seat and drove the car into a side street, got out and told Satch that he didn't ever want to see him driving in Cambridge again.

Then there was Satch's fear of the water—which he told us came from an experience he had one day at Coney Island. His mother, who was a great pal of everybody on the team, swears this story is true.

Satch and his mother went to the beach, and she got talking away with some other lady. Satch is all duded up, walking around, checking out the swimmers, and I'm sure the lady swimmers and the lady non-swimmers are getting the longest looks. He is standing at the end of the pier when he sees a rope hanging down from the pier into the water. Satch decides to see where the rope goes. So, clothes and all, he lowers himself down the rope. Next thing he knows he is sliding slowly down the rope, into the water. He keeps right on sliding, finally getting a good hold just before he runs out of rope. He hangs there for a bit, eyes wide open, realizing, as he said, that he is on the wrong end of the rope. He cannot swim a stroke. He can't pull himself back up the rope. He lets go of the rope, takes a guess as to which direction land is, and the minute his feet touch the sand, he starts walking as fast as he can. His mother said she was sitting on the beach and suddenly, the other lady pointed and here comes Satch striding out of the ocean. He always mentioned how lucky he was that he walked in the right direction. It was the first and last time Satch had anything to do with the water—except at Red's basketball camp where he tried to learn to swim with the help of six campers in two feet of water.

Still, it was Satch's driving experiences that provided an on-going situation comedy for us on the Celtics. When he asked me if I would teach him to drive, he told me I was the only one on the team with enough patience, which was probably true. Satch gave a good nudge to a telephone poll when we began our second lesson. We were using my car. Satch was immediately transferred to a drivers' education school in Cambridge.

When the day finally came for Satch to take his driving test, I agreed to be his sponsor. Many comments were made in the locker room when we left after practice to take the test. Satch drove the car over to Cambridge, and the motor vehicle office had a long lonely stretch of parking spaces in front of it. Satch gave me an old grin and said, "This is perfect. Pull right in here. Go get the man and zip right off."

We went inside to find the inspector, and when the three of us came out, Satch's fast pace slowed to a crawl. There were cars parked tightly in front of and behind our car. We got in with Satch behind the wheel, the inspector sitting in front beside him, and me in the back seat. Satch drove forward and back—forward and back. Maybe a dozen times Satch drove forward and back. I was biting on a handkerchief in the back. Finally the inspector leaned over and put his arm on Satch's shoulder. "If you don't turn the wheel," he said, "we will spend the entire day in this damn place."

We got out on the road and I was having an awful time trying to keep from laughing. Satch's eyes went from the road to the rear-view mirror, looking at me as I was rolling around the back seat—which is probably why Satch alternated between six and sixty miles an hour. Unfortunately, it was during the sixty mile an hour spin that he spotted a stop sign out of the corner of his eye after he had already passed it. When he hit the brakes, the inspector and I both ended up on the floor of the car. When the inspector got back up, he said in a very shaky voice, "We'll go back to the office now."

We got back and parked the car. There was a long silence as the inspector just sat in his seat. Satch said he knew his license was flying away somewhere over the roadways of Cambridge. But then he said he remembered where he was. He turned to the inspector and, in one of the great moments of his driving career, said, "Sir, I think it's wonderful that you're such a Celtics fan. I'd like to offer you two tickets for our playoff games. It would be my pleasure to have you there to see us play."

The inspector gulped and said, "Thank you, I appreciate that."

He signed Satch's license and handed it to him and said, "Here, take this, but you've got to promise me you'll go back to drivers' school."

That's what I call Celtics power.

I hope these stories are funny to somebody besides me. There are lots of them and they still give me a chuckle. I think for all of us they were as much a part of the Celtics experience as the games and the championships. I know that's still true now. As a coach, I miss taking part in a lot of that stuff, but I try to make sure I don't let it all pass me by. There's got to be some fun in what you do for a living or you ought to try and find something else to do. I've gone through my bleak time in basketball—it's fun for me again. When it stops, I'll stop.

I'm not planning to turn this into a joke book, but I think it's important that I give you a sense of the feeling of good fellowship that has always been part of being a Celtic. Maybe winning and feeling good are a kind of chicken and egg puzzle. If you don't feel good about one another—you won't win. And I'm sure that if you spend a season not winning—you won't feel good about one another. So, all of this is related to winning basketball games because in a curious way all of this adds up to creating a winning climate, and once you begin winning you build the psychology of a winner and you are tougher to beat. Players who stayed with the Celtics learned somehow that points are not the name of the game. Scoring is too often the most important part of the game for individual players on other teams. But the Celtics idea was dive for that loose ball, it belongs to us. Work hard moving the ball to get our real shooters open. Beat the opponent on the break, and if you get driven into the crowd as you shoot you don't lay around rubbing your aches and pains—you scramble to your feet and get back as fast as you can to play defense. Know the other team's weakness and work together to chop away at it. What we had on the court was total concentration and total hustle with one goal in mind— team victory. If the team is winning, you find time to have a laugh.

Laughter just doesn't seem right when you're losing.

C oncentration and attitude are two significant elements of our success then and now. You can't be scared or intimidated. That goes back to my thoughts on watching some of the rookies come into camp. I think the sad thing about some of them is that they are just plain scared and I don't believe you can achieve much of anything—on or off the basketball court—if you're running scared. That is one of the things that happened with the teams that played us then and with the teams that play us now. The Celtics are winners; we are successful. You can't be afraid to take the shot and miss it or to gamble on stealing the ball and lose. The Celtics are not afraid because they know their teammates will lend support and pick up the slack.

Another lesson I learned is that it's great to win, but bragging too much is not often wise. We were in a championship series with the Lakers. The first two games were in Boston and in the first game I did a real good job covering their wonderful shooter Jerry West. I held him to something like 16 points, and in the case of Jerry West, that was a real accomplishment. Afterward, the press crowded around my locker, something I wasn't used to. It seemed to me that every newspaper writer in the country was around my locker. They asked, "How did you stop the great Jerry West? What did you do to him? Can you tell us how you kept him in check?" Boy oh boy, that was heady stuff and I held court. I told them everything. "I did this and that and then a little bit more of the other." I really got carried away and I poured it on. Quiet K.C. let his tongue run away with his brain.

The next night Jerry West scored 43 points. I had forgotten that besides knowing what to do with the basketball, Jerry knew how to read. It taught me, or I should say re-taught me, a lesson that I was aware of: Be ever so humble when you're covering a super scorer. After shooting off my mouth—which is something I almost never did—I learned that silence is sometimes golden. But with the Celtics, there was only a grin and a little dig. We were all in it together and I wouldn't do it again and my teammates knew it. I shut my mouth and went back to playing the part that God and Red had chosen for me—and by the way, I must admit, I've never been certain that Red and God are two different people.

Maybe another story about one of my teammates would explain how we all came to understand our roles. In a strange way we learned what was expected of us almost without talking about it. I suppose it was a part of Red's genius as a coach—some magic communication method that he had—that caused all of us to sense what ingredient we were meant to supply to the team.

This is another story about my pal, Satch Sanders, who was a great defensive player, a hard rebounder and like everybody on our Celtics teams, an intense competitor. Satch didn't come to the Celtics as a defensive player. He had been a big star at New York University where he averaged 22-23 points a game. He was the Celtics' number one draft pick in 1960. I think he was in the top eight players in the country drafted that year. Red had something quite different in his mind than Satch expected. Red was going to make Satch a defensive part of the team. Funny how Red would draft a guy for defense. He drafted the great John Havlicek for defense. So, Satch became a defensive player and a superb one. He and I used to bet a beer or a coke or a dollar or occasionally, if Satch could find his wallet, we'd bet a dinner on who could do the best defensive job on the man we were going to play that particular night. Somehow or other Satch decided that being a great defensive player was not quite what he wanted to do. For a few games, the old Satchmo was cranking them up. Now, this is on a team that has some pretty fair country shooters—named Heinsohn, Cousy, Russell and Jones. Of course you understand, I am referring to Sam Jones. No one said a word. That was one of the great things about our Celtics teams and still is—there's no finger pointing and that keeps it a happy family. It's not a bad policy to follow in the rest of your life either.

One evening Satch scored 24 or 25 points. He really looked like a whiz out there, but the Celtics got beat. That happened two or three times during the next couple of weeks that Satch was on his shooting binge. No one said a word through all of this. I would guess that Red, being the genius that he is, was watching and waiting to see what happened. Then one night before a game, Satch suggested we have a little bet on who could play the best defense that night. He looked at me after he said it and gave me a grin and I knew that Satch must have had a little talk with himself. He was back in the role that would help the team the most. The Celtics got back to their winning ways—the family was back in sync.

I think that story illustrates a couple of things that people didn't fully appreciate about those teams that I was so lucky to be associated with. The players, without exception, were smart and tough. Satch was smart enough to figure out what the team needed most and tough enough to be able to give up headlines and glory and All Star teams to do the hard job that needed to be done to make us winners.

A natural part of sports talk seems to be comparing teams. The fans do it, the sportswriters do it and although some of them won't admit it, old time players do it too. Which team was the best? Could the team of such and such a year beat the team from another year? This year's Celtic team is talked about in terms of greatness or the greatest ever. People ask me how I compare this year's team with the teams that I played on. Well, first of all this year's team is bigger than our teams were. Right now, it's fresher. But as big as they are and as fresh as they are, our old teams would give them a hell of a game. Let's just leave it at that.

If a game could be concocted with both teams in their prime, there would be one mutual ingredient that would cause it to be quite a battle—that ingredient would be pride. Everybody who's worn or wears the Celtic uniform has that.

Although I can't give you a clear definition, that thing called Celtics Pride does exist. If I tried to express it in a few words, I think it would sound corny. It's much easier for me to tell you who created Celtics pride. Like the creation of a life it took two people—Red Auerbach and Bill Russell. I still get the feeling that the people of Boston never really understood what they had when Bill Russell was playing basketball for the Celtics. Red certainly did—and he told the world about it—and the players did.

Bob Cousy said it best. "Bill Russell revolutionized basketball. He changed the patterns of play both for individuals and for teams. First and foremost Bill Russell was a team man. The one who made us go. Without him we wouldn't have won a championship."

Cousy said it all—Russ was a team man. His contributions on the court were there for everybody to see. He made a greater contribution to a basketball team than had ever been made before. Russ could rebound and shot block better than anybody who ever played the game of basketball. He studied rebounding. His whole being concentrated on stopping his man's shot, on intimidating and on getting the ball after a shot. No one should ever forget that Bill's purpose in getting the ball was to give it to his teammates. Sure he took his shots—he had to to keep the other team honest. But no one ever accused Russ of being a great shooter. His goal was aiding his teammates and denying the other team victory.

That's what the fans saw on the court. Many of them appreciated it—every player in the league did.

With those of us who played with him, black and white, Bill was a thoughtful, giving man. Russ never looked down on the lowliest sub—and I've spent some time in that category. If you were broke, it was Russell who put some money in your pocket. If it was serious money, and sometimes it was with some of the guys, he would go and borrow the money for them. Many times I saw Russ sense that a player was down in the dumps—it might be a guy that he wasn't really tight with—and there they'd be, out to dinner with each other. With Russ picking up the tab. He gave everything he had in a game. We knew he expected to win every game. He had that confidence about him and transmitted it to us.

The public never saw much of the Mr. Nice Guy side of Russ but it was there and everybody on the team knew it. Perhaps I can sum up Celtic Pride by saying that Bill Russell taught us to believe that we were not just one person—each one of us had the strength and skill of the group. We were never alone on the court or in life. When the time came that my life went sour, when I was on a slide going down hill, there were Celtics that reached out to me and Bill Russell was one who reminded me that I was not alone.

I certainly wasn't alone my first year with the team. Russell, in typical fashion, insisted that I move in with him and his wife, Rose, in their home in Reading. I was more than glad to be able to do that. Having a bed at Russ' helped my wallet as well as my heart. Rose was a sweetheart. Many women would have been resentful at the fifth wheel being put on their shiny new car but not Rose. We became good pals—and we still are.

I won't tell you how much money I was being paid or you'll think this is all fiction. However, I will say that my annual salary probably would work out to about what Larry Bird gets for the time it takes him to lace up his sneakers. That first year my entire energy was directed toward making the team and staying on the team. Outside of phone calls and letters to Beverly I had very little communication with the outside world. Social life for Russ, Rose and me consisted of occasional visits to a place called The Big M on Mass Avenue in the South End of Boston. If you walked through the bar and did a broken field run through the crowd and went downstairs, you found yourself in a cool, shadowed room where you could sit and have a drink and listen to some velvety smooth music. The three of us enjoyed our nights there. There was D.D. Ford and Johnny Hammond Smith on the organ. He's the man who wrote the Marlboro music. The Big M featured some fine acts and it was nice to sit and relax with a beer and let the music float around you. For me that was the social side of Boston.

It isn't really completely accurate to say that I thought only of basketball that year. Beverly and I kept in touch with one another on the phone and through letters, and got to see one another when the team played in Chicago and Detroit. When the season ended I went out to Illinois and we were married. My mother and brother and sisters were there and both families hit it off fine. I knew that it was going to take lots of hard work to keep wearing that Celtics uniform. I was sure Beverly was the right partner for me to have in that effort, that we'd make a good team.

After that first season my hopes of staying with the Celtics, for at least another year, were high. Beverly and I settled into an apartment in the South End of Boston. I spent the summer as I have for almost every summer since—working at a basketball camp and spending some time beginning a love affair with that wonderful game called golf.

We won the 1959–1960 championship in a tough seven game series with St. Louis. So, I was two for two with the Celtics and it felt good, but what felt even better was being associated with people like Bob Cousy, Frank Ramsey, Bill Sharman, Tom Heinsohn, Sam Jones, Jim Loscutoff, Gene Conley, Ben Swain, Lou Tsioropoulos. Somehow all of these guys and myself managed to fit onto Russell's shoulders while the one and only Red pointed us all in the right direction and got us there. If it seems I've been complaining about the money I was paid for playing with these guys, then I'm not telling it quite right. The fact is, if I'd been a rich man, I would have paid money to be part of the group. You'll be tired of this if you get to the end of this book with me but I'll say it again, I believe the Celtics' success comes from the character of the people who began the winning tradition and those are the two big R's—Red and Russell.

Mentioning the friends I've played with and against over the years could fill a book all by itself. I think that's one of the special treats that goes with sports, no matter if it's Little League or Big League. I'm sure that all of you who have been involved in some kind of athletic competition at any level have made lifelong friendships with your teammates and with some of your competitors.

The suitcase situation of professional sports can get pretty tiring. Getting into and getting out of airports at all hours and in all types of nasty weather makes some guys look in the mirror and wonder if it's all worth it. I've never had that doubt and one of the reasons is that in traveling around this great country all my adult life, following the bouncing ball, I've been blessed in making many good friends off the court. Consequently, my life on the road with the team is a nice series of welcome backs.

For the first time in my life, I was sitting on the bench. I learned to get used to it because I sat on the bench for the next five years.

Buddy LeRoux, now part owner of the Boston Red Sox, tapes Bill Russell.

What great form!

I didn't do this often.

K.C. Jones going to the hoop in Boston Garden.

K.C. Jones going past the great Jerry West of the Los Angeles Lakers.

Red once said that when he put me into a game, things started to happen.

Bill Russell was a team man...He made a greater contribution to a basketball team than had ever been made before.

Tom Heinsohn, who later became a successful Celtics' coach, makes use of his patented hook shot.

John Havlicek studied and learned every aspect of the game. I never saw another player grow as steadily into greatness as he did.

K.C. Jones, Jerry West and Bill Russell on the court in Boston Garden.

K.C. Jones defending against the Detroit Pistons.

Chapter Nine

During the 1965–1966 season I began to think seriously about my future on and off the court. I knew I wasn't going to be able to keep running around in shorts in front of people all my life. The world had been very patient waiting for me, but I couldn't keep dodging the bullet forever. The Celtics had some players sitting on the bench who deserved more playing time. Larry Siegfried, a good defensive player and a better shooter than I was, was one of them. I knew that Siggy should be getting more minutes. It was important for the team.

One night a young rookie with the Sixers was bringing the ball up the court. He put a move on me and I reached out to sock the ball away from him and suddenly he went by me. I don't think anybody thought it was a big deal, but I did. I had been embarrassed on a basketball court while doing what I thought I could do better than anybody else—play defense. A few weeks later something similar happened. I didn't like it and I wasn't going to let it happen again. I told Red that I was going to hang it up. If I couldn't be at my best I didn't want to be on the court. Red was very upset. He said he wouldn't hear of me quitting. I told him I was really serious and he gave me a kind of a funny look and said he knew that I was and that he didn't like to hear it.

Around the same time I was approached by Brandeis University. They were looking for a head coach. I talked it over with Red and, as usual, we ended up doing it his way. That's not difficult for me to say because Red's way usually ends up being the smartest way. We decided that I would wait a year before going to Brandeis and I could recruit some players for the Brandeis team and play one last season with the Celtics. Funny, that last year was the only year in my nine years with the Celtics that we didn't win the championship. We got wacked four games to one by Philadelphia and when the series was over all the guys said, "Come on Case, one more year. We'll come back and win it again." I was very tempted, but I'd given my word to Brandeis, and there was still that business of not wanting to be embarrassed on the court. I knew in my heart that I couldn't do some things on the court as well or as fast as I'd been able to do eight years before, and the young players on the Celtics bench had shown that they were more than ready.

Still it hurt not to get one more ring. At that point in my basketball life I had been involved in two NCAA Championships, an Olympic Gold Medal team and eight NBA championships. All of those came one after the other. It wouldn't be an exaggeration to say that I had grown accustomed to winning.

When the Celtics announced that I was retiring, a lot of very nice people got together and had a night for me at the Garden. The place was full with a lot of good feelings coming from the crowd. Beverly and our children, my mother, and one sister were all there to share in this special moment.

When I was handed the microphone to speak I was really nervous. I remember one of the kids was holding onto my legs—I was glad she was because my knees were knocking. I wished that I could sing the people a song to express how I truly felt at that moment. Back then I was much more comfortable singing in public than I was at giving speeches.

One of the pats on the back I recieved was the Key to the City of Framingham. We had been living there since 1961 in a little house on Wayside Road that got more and more squeezed as our family grew. That gesture by the town of Framingham touched us because we were one of the few black families in the town.

Ironically, later when we tried to purchase another, larger home in Framingham, we made the mistake of assuming we could choose any neighborhood. We did have the Key to the City, but our realtor was told that the home we first chose was in an area with neighbors who did not want a black family moving there. This attitude still concerns me. Finally, we found another home in a different section of Framingham. This all happened in the late 60s. I'd like to think this wouldn't happen today.

I knew it was time for me to see how I could live outside of the Celtics family. I had traveled the world playing the hoop game. I had made my living in a pressure cooker but always as a team man with a team. Now I was on my own. I was a grown man with a wife and five children. They looked to me for guidance, but I was going to learn that sometimes the guide can lose his way.

I was going to have to supplement my salary with Brandeis—there was no doubt about that. Along came a fellow, who shall remain nameless, who offered me a chance to get into the insurance business. This seemed to be a line of work that would make sense for me. I think I'm pretty good one-on-one. So it seemed that if I could learn the insurance game I would have something that wouldn't depend on the ball going in the hoop. The idea came from a fellow who was a million dollar round-table type—a big success in the insurance business. We would work together. I was well aware of the fact that I didn't know the business. I would be with an experienced, successful insurance agent. I understood what they wanted from me. They were using me and my name. There were people I could contact and places I could get into because I was K.C. Jones of the Celtics. I figured that was fair enough. We weren't going to mislead anybody on the insurance details because I had this partner who knew it all—plus I believe in insurance. It seemed a reasonable approach for me to learn the business. I'd be like a cop on the beat: I wasn't going to be chief of police right away but if I kept pounding the beat, I could get there someday.

I want to make it clear that the fellow who ran the agency then and still does now was and is an on-the-level guy. We started off like a house on fire. The agency was very pleased. My new associate and I called on many people I knew or who knew me. The arrangement seemed to be going well until the day the head of the agency called me in to tell me that there were some bookkeeping problems. That's when the bottom fell out. It seems that my partner was either too good at what he was doing or not good enough. He made a quick exit from our partnership and there were people upset with K.C. Jones the insurance man. There was only one thing to do. I took the savings that Beverly and I had put together from the years of chasing the Jerry West's and the Elgin Baylor's and the Oscar Robertson's and paid back the money the people were owed. It was important to me to go back and see everyone I had dealt with and make things right. It was no great pleasure sitting in front of some angry people. This was a painful rookie year in business. I had allowed myself to be put in the position of a young fellow entering school as a senior instead of as a freshman, which is what I certainly was. Rather than pounding the beat and learning like a rookie, I was entering the doors of executive offices like an old pro. It was a mutual mistake. I didn't make the team as an insurance man. As far as making it in the business world, I went back to square one. It wasn't a happy experience to put it mildly, no doubt about it.

I do have a business venture now that really pleases me. I'm involved in the Tony Roma restaurant in, of all places, Framingham. This venture carries a great bonus because one of my partners is Bobby Orr, a man whom I admire as much as anyone I've ever met. A noble man. When you hear the name Bobby Orr, believe me you are hearing a name of absolute integrity.

I can't talk of integrity without mentioning another man, Thomas Satch Sanders, who also was put into the meat grinder of the business world right after he left the Celtics in a Boston restaurant called Satch's. The restaurant, located just off Copley Square, was an attempt to create a place where blacks and whites could share equal time at the bar and at the table. Many creative partners were involved at the beginning of that venture, but they found that either Boston or the world wasn't ready for the idea. As it got tougher and tougher most of Satch's partners just drifted away. Satch was practically living in the place, working almost twenty-four hours a day to keep it going. He wasn't even drawing a salary out of the deal; he was just trying to pay his bills fairly. People advised him to shut the door and walk away himself, but that's not his way. It wasn't on the basketball court or in his life. When Satch's finally did close, Satch left the venture with his head held high and the absolute respect of the people who had come in contact with him.

That was Satch's second bad break in a short space of time. The first one was being picked to coach the Celtics at a time when both the direction of the team and player personnel had been taken out of Red's hands by an owner whose ego almost destroyed the Celtics. But that's a story we'll talk about later.

Anyhow, there I was, a failed insurance man and a rookie coach at Brandeis University. Brandeis was an important stop in my life's travels. If I hadn't coached there I wouldn't be coaching the Celtics. The kids at Brandeis were student-athletes and you could say my time there was spent being an athletic student—I was learning to be a coach and there was plenty to learn. The first lesson was that I was K.C. Jones, not Red Auerbach.

I had just spent nine intense years playing for Red and I suppose it was natural for me to think, "Well, there's Red, the most successful pro coach there ever was. What I better do is use the same tactics that made Red successful."

Red could have the sharpest tongue imaginable. He could bring a player to the point of tears. In fact, I used to watch in wonder when he would verbally savage Tom Heinsohn. I wondered what would happen if Heinie picked up Red and stuffed him in the hoop, because he could have. But Heinie would stand silently and take it like a school boy who'd misbehaved.

So, I did a bit of the sharp tongue stuff myself on the Brandeis kids and, of course, it was wrong—mainly because that's not me. I think a coach is at his best when his players are getting the honest to God, real character of a man. Those kids didn't deserve my theatrics. My only excuse is, we were both learning. Brandeis is a top notch educational institution, and the Brandeis players were students first. There was none of this stuff you hear today about how in some schools the players don't know where the classrooms are. That's not the way it was at Brandeis then, and you may be sure it's not now. I suppose one possible way to prove that I was dealing with student-athletes is to tell you that the team record was seven wins and thirty-four loses in the two years before I became coach.

Recruiting for Brandeis wasn't easy. The kids' grades had to be above average and almost without fail they would ask, "Where is it?" For those of you who don't know, Brandeis University is in Waltham, Mass. It was established as a Jewish oriented university and often a prospective student-athlete or his parents would ask if you had to be Jewish or become Jewish. That was an easy one, and I could use my own experience with the Jesuits at USF where you didn't have to be a Catholic to get an education. All in all, Brandeis was not exactly what you'd call a recruiter's dream, but I was lucky to have some terrific kids. We had a player named Bruce Singal who was a Satch-type player, a real scrapper who gave all he had every minute.

Another one of my players at Brandeis was Mark Shulman. Handling Mark put one of the early pages in my coaching handbook. He was a player who gave me a lot of input as far as the team was concerned. He suggested bringing up a freshman because he realized the freshman could handle the ball well and help the team. Mark himself was a scrappy player and a great shooter. But I felt he had some weaknesses on defense and his rebounding needed more work. As the season progressed his playing time was limited. One day he asked to meet with me and told me he was leaving the team. He said he felt there had been situations where he could have been productive against other teams but he wasn't used. His dad had come up to see us play a game against Maine and he and his dad discussed the situation after the game. They decided he was going to leave the team. I tried to talk him out of it, but his mind was made up. I should have used Mark Shulman differently. That situation was the beginning of my understanding that you should use a player's strengths and try to have other players compensate for his weaknesses. When a player is going to the trouble to give the coach thoughtful input, the coach should listen and analyze it.

This year before our sixth and final game with Houston I sought out Dennis Johnson and Robert Parish and sat down with them individually to get their thoughts on what we should do to handle the Houston team. It was clear that if Houston beat us in Boston in the sixth game, they would be an awful handful in a seventh game. Dennis and Robert gave me some real help in analyzing the situation. That's what Mark Shulman was trying to do at Brandeis.

All the Brandeis kids carried heavy study loads. Often we'd have lots of absentees at practice time due to labs or extra study for tests. It never bothered me a bit. I respected the kids for what they were doing. Basketball at Brandeis was meant to be fun for the players and I hope it was. I enjoyed it and I learned from it, but I didn't have the coach's mentality yet. I believe I improved their program. Our record after three years was thirty-five wins and thirty-two loses. At that time Bob Harrison, the coach at Harvard, asked me to come there as his assistant. Just before that I had been approached by the Atlanta Hawks about becoming an assistant coach with them. I turned down that opportunity because I felt I wasn't ready. Brandeis had taught me that I had lots to learn before I got to where I wanted to be in the coaching world. I thought that spending some time with players at a Division One school, and especially a Harvard would help me learn to be a coach. I figured I'd better learn coaching because it was crystal clear that I wasn't going to be an insurance man.

When I left Brandeis I wrote them a letter and thanked them for the many kindnesses I received there. I told them that I was sorry that I hadn't done a better job for them.

I can't really call this part of the book "K.C. Goes to Harvard." I stayed clear of the classrooms, but a close look at an Ivy League sports situation was interesting. First there was the coach, Bob Harrison, the man who asked me to be his assistant, one of the best guys and best coaches I've ever worked with. Talk about communicating.

He was a coach who related to his players. I remember once when a player's car broke down some place in the boonies in the middle of the night. He called Bob and the coach got in his car and went out and rescued the man. That's the kind of guy he was.

And the talent—there was plenty there. James Brown, who is now a television commentator, was a fine player, and another young man named Floyd Lewis. Those two and some of the others could have played for anybody, anywhere.

A lot of people at Harvard looked down at their athletes. This surprised me because they had some good ones and I thought they should be proud of them. I don't know what the situation is now, but when I was there, they seemed to be especially embarrassed that they had a basketball team. Football was O.K. It created a very social situation that everybody seemed to like, but basketball was not that popular.

A big flap came up while I was there. The student newspaper climbed all over Bob Harrison. The issue was race. The paper said Bob was favoring black players over white players. So in that case we had the white coach accused of favoring the black players. This year it was the David Thirdkill/Rick Carlisle issue, K.C. favoring a white player over a black player. What does it all mean? Not much, other than things don't change. The racial hammer can hit in both directions. The best we can do is take the whacks when they come and try and keep on going. I didn't have to learn that lesson at Harvard but I did see what the media could do to a good coach and a good man. That was a lesson I should have paid more attention to.

E ducation at Brandeis and Harvard turns out many rich graduates, but for a fellow learning the coaching profession at those schools, the paychecks are pretty slim. The Jones family had grown steadily. The house in Framingham was full. We had five children—Leslie, Kipper (K.C. Jr.), Kelly, Bryna and Holly. Five terrific kids and not such a terrific bank balance.

We spent our summers together at a basketball camp at Norwich University in Vermont, and I hope those were happy times for the kids. My wife did a great job with our children. I don't ever remember her complaining about the lack of money. She was a rock during the insurance disaster and as I tried to climb up the basketball coaching ladder she watched me change jobs and always cheered me on. The fact is, those were troubled times for us financially.

Near the end of the season at Harvard I got a call from Fred Schaus, the general manager of the Los Angeles Lakers. He asked me if I would like to become assistant coach to Bill Sharman, my old Celtics teammate, who had just been named head coach of the Lakers. I told Bob Harrison about the offer and being the kind of guy he was, he said, "Hey, go to it."

Beverly was pleased too. We both were getting more concerned with the kids trying to live in an all white society. She packed our bags and we were off to L.A. It seemed to me that going to the coast, we were going to the right place at the right time.

Chapter Ten

've always been willing to work my way up. My approach of going from cop on the beat to chief of police hadn't worked in the insurance business, but I hoped I could make it happen in the basketball world. People could fool me about business matters, but I knew they couldn't kid me about any business on the basketball court. That doesn't mean that I expected to be a head coach in the NBA—I didn't. I reasoned that the Lakers experience would put me in line for a major college coaching job, where I could spend my life with some financial security and the challenge of top level college basketball.

I don't think I would have taken the job with the Lakers if Bill Sharman hadn't been coach. I knew I still had a lot to learn about coaching. My original strategy back then was to stay awhile at Harvard and get a close look at Division One basketball. But the offer from L.A. attracted me because of who was Head Coach. Bill Sharman was someone I felt comfortable with. I knew Bill well from our Celtics days. We had spent years killing one another in practice. He was competitive and determined. I knew what a quiet, steady man he was and I felt good about working for him. I had great respect for him. Otherwise, I was nervous as hell about being the assistant coach of the Lakers. This was a fabulous team of Hall of Fame caliber players. I was nervous about dealing with these stars. I knew the Lakers were not a humble group but IBM isn't humble either. Why should they be?

As I think about life in the NBA, I don't think you can be a great player and be humble—certainly not on the court. On and off the court, the Lakers had great confidence. I guess some of that flair comes from living and playing in L.A. For myself, the Boston scene was and is less intense off the court and much more comfortable than the Hollywood situation.

The Lakers had assembled a squad that included Elgin Baylor, Jerry West, Gail Goodrich, Keith Erickson, Jimmy McMillan, Pat Riley, the current Lakers coach—a terrific coach, by the way—was one of the hard nosed men who came off the bench, Happy Hairston was there and the biggest name of all, the lightning rod that everyone talked about, the players watched, the media wrote about and the photographers focused on, the strongest big man that ever played the game—Wilt Chamberlain. Think of this—Wilt Chamberlain's upper arm measured twenty three inches around—he is 7'2" tall—he weighed 310 pounds, and could run like a gazelle. Run that around in your mind for a bit.

I had never thought much of Wilt as a winning player or as a team man. We'd been in some fierce games with him when I was with the Celtics and he was in Philly. There was always too much controversy around him and therefore around the team. I figured he caused it. Philly had a team that should have been able to beat the Celtics most times but they couldn't. Without ever saying so out loud, I unfairly blamed Wilt for this at the time.

Bill Sharman was everything I thought he would be. He was a perfectionist and a workaholic. He had a very quiet approach to the game. He listened to the players and respected their ideas. These days I get a kick out of watching Raymond Berry of the Patriots writing down notes during his team's games. Bill Sharman was the original Mr. Notes. He wrote down every little detail that caught his eye.

Before the first practice Bill and I were standing together talking and one of our players walked by and said, "The big guy's not going to give it to you." Sharman and I stared at one another. We didn't say a word but I can tell you the remark blew my mind. If Wilt was going to dog it we were in for a long season. We did lose our first two games, but then Wilt turned things around for us. I could see that Wilt Chamberlain was giving us one hundred percent. He practiced hard and he played hard but we were losing. Some of the other players were just beginning to learn their roles on the team.

Bill Sharman sat the team down and he let them have it bit by bit, point by point. He chewed them up one side and down the other. Not wild and wooly yelling but hard, no nonsense coaching. He told them that what's not there is what's supposed to be there. When he got through everybody in that room knew what was expected of them. He detailed every man's role exactly. I figured I was a lucky man to be in that room and watch Bill Sharman do his thing. What a coach! What a man!

We started to win and as that team played winning basketball I watched Wilt Chamberlain and my respect for him grew and grew. Wilt was the guy the papers and the fans always hammered on. The the media made him a villain and he never seemed to be able to turn that image around. If the team lost it was going to be his fault. If the team won it was almost as if the team won even though he played for them. I decided that the controversy in Philly and their failure to win were someone else's fault. Wilt worked so hard and wanted so much to win. And strong, Mercy! I've never seen anybody like him. I remember Russell saying that the first time he played against Chamberlain, Wilt and he grabbed an offensive rebound at the same time and when Wilt went up to the hoop with the ball Russell thought, "My God, he's gonna stuff me and the ball into the hoop." To play with Wilt was the chance to play with a dominator. As I look back on it now, I think maybe some of his teammates resented that rather than respected it.

The winning streak continued. The players began to fit comfortably into their roles. It was like old times with the Celtics. Bill Sharman had told these guys what it meant to be a team and the players responded. Jerry West, a beautiful shooter, played defense like Larry Bird does today. Gail Goodrich brought the ball up with the smarts and savvy of Dennis Johnson and, like Dennis, he was an unselfish player. Happy Hairston became a great offensive rebounder.

The Lakers won thirty-three games in a row. Obviously everybody was playing great basketball. Wilt was a demon on the court. We got to Milwaukee—Kareem was with them then—and the streak was broken that night.

The season rolled on and as it did our life in L.A., like the basketball world, was a comfortable one. The kids were in schools that had a little bit of everything and everybody. It was kind of a replay of my trip from Texas to San Francisco. My kid's reaction was, "Wow, look at all these black people. Look at all these Mexicans. Look at all these Japanese." They were getting their first look at the real world. It didn't seem to phase them.

That season was going well. It was good enough even for the L.A. fans. The season record was an awesome sixty nine wins and thirteen loses—which I think is still a record. In fact when the media talks about this year's Celtics team being the best ever, perhaps they should take a look at that L.A. team. They might even take a peek at some old

Celtics teams.

Sometimes in the course of a long season you can pinpoint one or two or maybe a few occasions that are crucial for the team's success for the year. This year more than one or two games were vital for the Celtics, but a few stand out. The first happened on Christmas Day, when we led the Knicks by twenty-five points in the third quarter and ended up losing 113–104 in a double overtime. The game was on national television, so every one of us knew that not only had we played poorly, but we had also embarrassed ourselves from coast to coast. Perhaps in a strange way that game was almost a blessing. After the game I talked to the team without any shouting. I have too much respect for my players to handle even that kind of a disaster that way. I believed there was no way this team was going to let that happen to them again.

Another key moment for us in the year happened down in Atlanta in the last part of January. The Hawks were on a roll, playing well. They had won a bunch of games in a row when we got down there. They were very cocky and there was a lot of talk on the court. At half time they were way out in front of us. Looking at the guys in the locker room, I saw some cold, hard eyes. I didn't have to say much. I just told them that I wanted them to do some different things on defense. In the third quarter we stopped the Hawks in their tracks. Larry played as only he can and especially as he can if he thinks someone is trying to make a fool of him or the team—and remember I'm sure that in his mind he and the team are one. I mean that as the highest compliment I can pay. We beat the Hawks in overtime by three points. I have no doubt that the results of that game affected both teams. I think that game had an impact on Atlanta as a team.

Beating L.A. out there and at home were ballgames that were very significant to both teams this year. I'm not going to say much more than that because as I said earlier, I know all those guys can read.

For the 1971–1972 Lakers, the key game was having the streak broken in Milwaukee with Jabbar leading the way. There was no question then that one of us was going to win it all. When we met them in the playoffs, they took us to six games. Before the series and again before the sixth game, Wilt came to me and we spent lots of time discussing how he should play Jabbar. In that sixth game victory, Wilt carried the team on his back in one of the greatest one man performances I've ever seen. After that we met New York in the finals and blew them away four games to one. I had another championship ring. This one said Los Angeles Lakers. Don't ever think that life is predictable.

How good was that team? Good enough that Jimmy McMillian replaced Elgin Baylor in the lineup and averaged better than eighteen points a game. Elgin, the legend, retired before the season was over. His knees were giving him terrible pain. I wished he'd stayed with us until the end but I could understand how a man like Elgin would never want to play at less than his best.

Not all teams are alike in the way they handle playoff shares. That particular year with the Lakers, the player representative came in to see Bill Sharman and suggested that because Bill was head coach, management should pay his share of the playoff winnings. This was an unusual move in my experience. In those days, the players on winning teams traditionally sat down and divvied up their winning money, portioning one share to the coach. That the players' rep would come to the head coach and suggest that they weren't going to include him in the split and that he should ask management for the money after the year we'd had shocked me. When I told my old Celtics pals about this, we all hooted with laughter as we tried to figure out who would have had the guts to go in and give that little piece of news to Red.

Yes, sometimes this whole process of splitting up the playoff purse needs a Solomon-like judge.

Fortunately, we had one in the 1965–1966 season when I was playing in Boston. That year, we finished behind Philly in the NBA East and ended up winning the championship. When it came time to talk about dividing the money, we had a team meeting in a room in the old Madison Hotel next to the Boston Garden. Naturally the Celtics didn't have a meeting like other teams with just the players there. Our meeting included Red and Buddy LeRoux, the trainer.

Somehow, some chatter developed regarding the amount that Woody Sauldsberry and John Thompson should receive. Woody had missed half the season with an injury. John Thompson, now the great Georgetown coach, was the back-up center for Russell. In that position you got to spend a lot of time on the pine. Somebody suggested that Woody and John get half shares. John spoke up and said, "Russ, you're the forty eight minute man and even though I haven't logged a lot of minutes, I've been ready to play all year. So if you guys don't think I'm worth a full share, I'm not taking a half share. Give Woody a full share."

I could feel the guys thinking, "What the heck are we doing?" As usual Russell was one step ahead of us, and make no mistake, even though Red was there, Russ was in charge of that meeting. He stood up, waved a long arm and said, "The hell with that kind of stuff, everybody gets a full share."

We didn't need to have a vote—that was the end of the meeting. Incidentally, that insightful performance by John Thompson should give you some idea why he's the dedicated, disciplined, successful coach he is.

The 1971–1972 year with the Lakers was a good one for all the Jones family. Working with Bill Sharman was an experience I'll never forget. I thought Bill was a beautiful person when I went out to the coast to work for him. By the end of the season, I was sure of it.

Bill Sharman wasn't the only ex-Celtic on the West Coast who helped me make a smooth transition into pro coaching. Another old buddy who continues to keep in touch to this day is Willie Naulls. I stayed with Willy before Beverly and the kids arrived on the coast. He was right there everytime we needed something. Like the great player he was, he even anticipated some of our needs before we even knew about them. He is a success story that I love to talk about. I've known him through a lot of seasons. In our College days when USF made the trip to South America, Willie came with us. He had some great years with St. Louis, San Francisco and the Knicks, and when it looked as though his career was coming to a close, Russell suggested to Red that we try to sign him.

Willie was astonished by the Celtics approach. As I said earlier, he collapsed at our first season practice after about a half hour. He was carried off the court and placed on the trainer's table. When he came around, his first words were, "I'm going home—this is too much work." His astonishment continued through his seasons with us. He said that with other teams, when the ball came down the floor you could be all alone, waving and doing a war dance under the hoop and you wouldn't get the ball. The players would say, "It's not your turn. Next time we come down the court we'll give you a chance to take a shot."

Willie Naulls was a good shooter. He learned very quickly that with the Celtics the open man gets the shot. We *want* the shooter to take his shot. A good illustration of that for Willie happened in one of his first playoff games with us. During a time out we all walked toward the bench while Russell turned around and went over to Sam Jones, who was trudging up the court, "Why didn't you take that last shot?" Russ asked him.

"Hell, I've missed six shots in a row, I'm just not hitting," Sam said.

"Listen," Russ said, "you are the best shooter in the world. I don't care if you miss sixty shots in a row. You got the shot, take it. That's what we all want you to do."

Willie had never heard that kind of talk before.

Willie played almost five hundred games with other professional teams, but he is proudest of his three years with the Celtics. Over the mantlepiece in his beautiful house in Los Angeles is a large painting of five Celtics with their heads together on the court. There is Russ, Satch, Sam Jones, Willie and myself. Five black men. We were the first NBA team to put five black men on the floor at once. We are all proud of that; that "we" includes Red, the spirit of Walter Brown and I'll bet everybody that's ever worn a Celtics uniform.

Willie told me once that during his big money days in basketball he headed east for training camp and realized he was broke. He had to borrow some cash from a friend and sleep on his couch. He vowed that would never happen to him again. It won't. Willie bleeds green. He said when his playing days were over he was going to go back to L.A. and "marry" the smartest business man he could find. He believed that was the best way to enter business. As a result of a profitable partnership and learning process, Willie is one of the most successful former professional athletes I know. Once he got to the top, he began a series of community service projects for minorities that continues today. I trust him and respect him. He acted as my advisor when the next door of opportunity opened for me—that door was in San Diego.

B y the early 1970's professional basketball was really getting a hook into American sports fans. Seeing a great opportunity, some wealthy individuals got together and started a new league—the American Basketball Association. The league started off pretty well, well enough that the owners decided to expand. San Diego was awarded a franchise. Dr. Bloom, a dentist, was the owner, and he hired Alex Groza, former Kentucky star, as his general manager. Alex contacted me and asked me to meet with him to discuss my being head coach of the San Diego team, the Conquistadors. In our very first meeting, I realized that Doc Bloom had more self-confidence than William F. Buckley. That didn't bother me—I was used to dealing with self-confident people.

The San Diego situation intrigued me. I talked it over with Bill Sharman. Bill was honest as always. He suggested that I stay with the Lakers and indicated that when he was finished I might become the Lakers head coach. He also said that he didn't think I was quite ready yet, and that another couple of years in LA would make a big difference. I appreciated Bill's remarks and I wonder now as I think back on that what would have happened if I had stayed. K.C. Jones—coach of the Lakers! Mercy!

But the truth is—I never dwell on the past. What's happened has happened and right now I'm coaching the Celtics.

Back then I decided I wanted to take on the San Diego challenge. San Diego is one of the great places in America to live, and living there at that time was one of the truly great guys of America—my old USF coach, Phil Woolpert. Phil had moved down the coast to become athletic director at San Diego State. It was nice to know that there would be a fine human being like Phil around with whom I could sit and talk. Alex Groza was also the kind of a guy that I felt would be a pleasure to work with.

The family packed up again and did all those things that were becoming second nature to us by now, while I wrestled with making a successful start as a head coach in the pros.

We started off with a try-out camp. Stan Albeck had been hired as my assistant. One hundred and twenty five players had been invited to try out. We didn't have a lot of time to study the players, but we put a squad together and got down to business.

The first half of the year went well. As an expansion team we surprised everybody—including myself. The team spent some time in first place. In the second half of the season injuries struck us, as one player after another got hurt. The wrath of Doc Bloom also struck when we lost sixteen games in a row. Coaches, even rookie head coaches, don't really have to learn about injuries. Everyone in the sports world knows that injuries are a part of the game just as disappointments are a part of life. Sometimes, though, injuries come like the rain. Everybody seems to get a bit of it. When this happens, a team's prospects for the season can change overnight. Injuries can level any team, and that's what happened in San Diego. I suppose it taught me a lesson about what can happen to some owners when their team goes on a losing streak. Doc Bloom decided he was going to straighten out the team. He ordered daily breakfast meetings consisting of Alex Graza, Stan Albeck, himself and yours truly. Doc Bloom was very grouchy at these meetings. They certainly didn't make my day. We wanted badly to turn things around and get back on track. Alex, Stan and I laughed about these breakfast meetings years later but they weren't very funny at the time.

Our good first half of the season gave us a record with enough clout to make the playoffs, but the team was not really at full strength. We were eliminated by the Utah team. Our season record was a losing one—the first time I had ever been involved with more defeats than victories in my professional life. I hope it's the last time. As luck would have it, not long after another door opened—back East again.

Chapter Eleven

Abe Pollin had become the owner of the Baltimore-based NBA team renamed the Capitol Bullets. Not long after the ABA season ended he called me. Abe was an upfront guy beginning with that first conversation. He said he had been impressed with the job that I had done that year with San Diego and wanted me to become head coach of his club. I was pleased at what he said because I felt that in spite of the Conquistadors' losing record, we had gotten as much out of the situation that season as could be had. To my surprise—and despite the unhappy breakfast meetings—Doc Bloom must have thought so too. When I told him that Abe Pollin had talked to me about the NBA job Doc Bloom told me in no uncertain terms that he wanted me to stay in San Diego.

It was not a difficult decision. I only had a one year contract with San Diego. That year was up. I was going to become an ex-Con. I had no doubt in my mind now that I could coach in the NBA. Somehow the losing in San Diego taught me as much as the winning in LA. I'm sure the year I spent as Bill Sharman's assistant made that happen. I knew that I could reach players by treating them with dignity and respect. I was able to watch a player and use his strengths for the team and have the team shore up his weaknesses. The time was right. My years of hard work on the basketball court, my hours of studying and analyzing the game seemed to be bearing a fruit that I never thought I'd taste. These were opportunities that were beyond my imagination as a black kid in Texas or a silent high school kid living at Double Rock in San Francisco.

My mother watched all this with quiet pleasure. She had seldom missed a high school game. In our big games against Commerce or Mission, she'd be right there—never shouting—but always there. She never quit being my fan. As the years went along she got the idea that if you played basketball you lived out of a suitcase. Now she wasn't surprised to learn that if you coached, you lived the same way. She had been pleased that we were on the West Coast, but she accepted the fact that we were leaving her to go back across the country. She didn't complain.

Before I left the West Coast, I had a reunion with my oldest, dearest buddies from junior high school—Ike Walker, and Charlie and McKinley Boyd. We reminisced about the old days back in the Hunter's Point projects. We recalled one night when we were coming home from a party together and a gang of five jumped out at us and told us to freeze.

We could see their purpose and were all shaking, knowing a battle was coming. Then the biggest guy stepped out to give a command and McKinley recognized him as someone he knew slightly.

"Gory," he bellowed. "Gory, Gory, it's me, it's me!"

"Oh, it's McKinley," the big guy said. "These guys are alright."

We didn't wait a half second to let them change their minds; we set records for the fast break and never stopped until we reached home.

I always remember the three-on-three games we played together, and I've never stopped seeing these dear friends whenever I visit the West Coast.

We packed up again and were off to Columbia, Maryland. We still spent our summers in the Northeast. I had become involved with a hard working, energetic teacher from Chelmsford, Massachussetts named Alex Robinson. We ran summer basketball camps in up-state New York and Vermont.

That summer of 1973 was a hectic one. After I signed as head coach of the Washington team it was my responsibility to pick an assistant coach. Stan Albeck and I had worked very well together in San Diego. He had a good feel for the game and I respected his talents. I offered him the job as my assistant but he chose to stay with Doc Bloom as head coach in San Diego.

During the year we spent in San Diego my ex-coach and always friend, Phil Woolpert, made a major decision about his life. He gave up his job as athletic director at San Diego State. Bang —just like that. He said thanks but no thanks to the California culture and he was gone. He moved to Squam, Washington. If you hear that name, I don't have to tell you how big the town is. Phil drives a school bus there and lives a very quiet life. I see him occasionally when the Celtics are up that way. He came down to San Francisco just this year at my request and presented me when I was inducted into the San Francisco Hall of Fame. I'm sure there is a better book in Phil Woolpert's life than there is in mine.

Bernie Bickerstaff had been a player for Phil and now coached basketball for him at San Diego State. I liked Bernie's style and enjoyed bouncing the conversational basketball around with him. I was interested in hiring the coach at Arizona named Fred Snowden, as my assistant. I decided to talk it over with Bernie since he had had experience against Snowden's teams. We sat in a cafeteria drinking coffee and discussed Snowden and what I expected from an assistant coach. While we were talking I said to Bernie, "Would you be interested in this job?"

"Wow!" Bernie said and kind of stood up out of his chair. "Are you kidding? You bet I would."

We didn't know it at that moment, but Bernie and I were headed for some hard times on the East Coast. He is a super guy and was a fine assistant coach and is now the head coach of Seattle. He is a fine basketball man but I don't tend to think of him so much as a basketball associate—because of our days in Washington, I tend to think of him more like a military buddy. It's as though we went through a war together.

While I was on the West Coast hiring Bernie, Abe Pollin was on the East Coast hiring Bob Ferry to be general manager of the Bullets. It would be the four of us, much more than the athletes, who would decide my destiny in the years of winning and losing with the Bullets.

I liked what I saw when I began with the Bullets. Actually, a more accurate statement would be that I liked what I felt. After dealing with the players for a short time, I came to believe that we had the makings of a team with good chemistry. I will always believe that good chemistry is more important than all the x's and o's that have ever been chalked on a board.

The Bullets had talent, not overwhelming talent, of course, but I thought the players were willing to pay the physical price necesary to succeed and the intellectual price that makes you think of the team first and brings victory.

We certainly didn't have a lot of height. Our twin towers were 6"9", Elvin Hayes and 6'7", Wes Unseld. Even in those days they could not be considered real big, but they were two powerful men who gave everything they had. Now it seems funny to call Wes Unseld a big man. He was always refered to that way when he played and in my mind he always will be. Wes Unseld was 6'7", and although a lot of guys are 6'7" tall, not many are also 6'7" wide. Wes knew how to use his body. He could set a numbing pick and was a relentless rebounder. Someone said that moving Wes out from under the hoop was like trying to move a huge truck with flat tires.

Elvin Hayes was a legitimate well-rounded star. He could do it all—shoot, rebound, block shots—all of it.

Those were our two big men.

Today when the Celtics put a big man lineup on the floor we might be talking Parish, McHale, Walton, Kite, none of whom is under 6'11". I suppose we could play Larry at guard and have him bring the ball up and he could be our small man and penetrating guard at 6'9". And you know what? Larry could do it too. Has the game changed? Well it certainly seems that there are more big fellows around these days.

With the Bullets in 1974 our penetrator and play-maker was Kevin Porter, and the other guard was a great sharpshooter, Phil Chenier. Mike Riordan was a defensive forward and I would bring rookie Nick Weatherspoon off the bench. He was probably as hot a streak-shooter as I have ever seen.

This was the nucleus of the team we put together in Washington. Each of the players had particular skills, and I felt that I was ready to direct the use of those skills. As I watched the team from the earliest practices, I knew that if I succeeded in teaching the players their roles the team could make good basketball music. Very few players can do it all. It's important to get the player who has one strength to concentrate intensely on the most valuable use of that strength in a game. At the same time the player should always be practicing just as intensely to develop additional skills.

Beverly and the kids seemed comfortable in Columbia. The community had a good school system and the kids were making friends, both black and white. I was completely absorbed in my job. I knew I had turned a lot of pages in the coaches' handbook. I felt very confident about the future of the team. I would try to teach them the same team-pride that I had learned with the Celtics and watched Bill Sharman create with the Los Angeles Lakers.

We played our games at the Capitol Center in Landover, Maryland, a nineteen thousand seat building that some sportswriters refer to as a cave. Capitol Center was built in the middle of a bean patch, but that didn't keep the fans away. As our first year progressed we were filling all nineteen thousand seats every night.

The staff at the Capital Centre was more than helpful and friendly to me. One special friend, Hymie Perlo, worked in community relations, and we always managed to have a few laughs together. We socialized quite a bit, and often he was a needed sounding board for me, always lightening up the conversation with his fine sense of humor. I have very fond memories of Hymie.

The Bullets were a good team when I got there, and they got better. Our first year together the team played almost six hundred percent basketball. It took the New York Knicks seven tough games to beat us in the Eastern semi-finals. The Celtics then beat the Knicks and ended up winning the championship. By the time the playoffs were over, I had no doubt that we had the respect of everyone in pro basketball.

As that season moved along and the chemistry between the team and the coach grew, so did the relationship between the coach and the owner. Abe Pollin became more than the owner. He was a friend and I think we both viewed our professional and social relationships in that light.

With Bob Ferry, our general manager, my relationship was one of mutual respect and the business of winning. That's as it should be. We became very involved in putting together the pieces of a winning team. I felt we could feel we had arrived and become complacent. We had to continue to improve to be competitive in our division. We were all eager for the next season to begin. If Mr. Injury stayed away from our door next year was going to be an exciting year for us. I thought we might please the owner, the general manager and the fans by putting championship rings on our players' fingers.

Sometimes — more than sometimes — reporters will ask me about my relationship with Red Auerbach. More than once a week I'll get a question about how much Red has to do with coaching the team or directing the team or deciding on players. Quite often the question is asked as though they hoped I would say, "What do you mean Red, he's retired from coaching. I'm the coach. I'm the man here. I don't need Red's help now."

Human nature being what it is, some of the media people seem a little disappointed when I give them my answer, which is, "I use Red's knowledge and wisdom every chance I get."

I imagine even the greatest writers have to turn to a research book once in awhile. They are in the business of writing and they want to do it the best way they can. I'm in the business of coaching professional basketball. I want to be as good as I possibly can be at that. I have the finest research book in the game available to me. That's Red. He's an encyclopedia of basketball. I listen to him and take advantage of his knowledge. I was doing it even back then with the Bullets.

I ran the same kind of early practices that Red always ran. I used the word "ran" twice in that sentence and it's appropriate because that's what we did. We ran and ran and ran in our early season practices. When the season started, we ran away from everybody in our division.

The Celtics were doing the same thing that year in their division. We matched them stride for stride as the year went on. Both teams ended with identical records—sixty and twenty-two. The Bullets finished nineteen games ahead of Houston in the Central Division.

I was very proud of our team. I had made a living in professional basketball by playing the toughest defense I could and by being an unselfish offensive player. That's the kind of team the Bullets were. We played grouchy, scratchy, face to face defense—the kind that forces your opponent to make mistakes. When they did, we turned it into a sizzling fast-break. All the players knew their roles and they were happy with them. Our home record that year was thirty-six and five, and that matched the record set by the great Lakers team that I had assisted in coaching.

The second season is the important one in professional basketball. We won the first one, but if you don't win the second, there is no cigar.

We started off against Buffalo in the playoffs. They really stretched us, but we won the series in seven games. There was not too much cheering at the end of that seventh game, however. We were headed for Boston Garden to play the World Championship Celtics who had just demolished the Houston Rockets.

Chapter Twelve

guess we could call this next little part of the book, "The Kid Comes Home."

The 1974-1975 Celtics were a fine team—a team with players named Havlicek, Cowens, White, Silas, Westphal, Nelson and Chaney. They had a brilliant coach who was as competitive on the bench as he had been on the court. Tom Heinsohn.

The Celtics had won the championship the year before in a show stopper series against Milwaukee and a young Jabbar. They had the same team back and they weren't really older—they were just smarter. Everybody expected them to repeat their performance.

The night of the opener I was proud to take the Bullets onto the Garden floor. Even though I was with the enemy, the Boston fans were nice to me. Well, almost. I don't know whether I looked nervous or calm on the outside, but a lot was going on in the inside.

The truth is, the kid did not think his team could beat the Celtics and the kid was working very hard to make sure nobody else knew that.

From the opening tap it was obvious that the Bullets didn't know I was worried. The Celtics had a 55-43 half-time lead. They had played great basketball, but our guys hadn't quit. We had a quiet half-time chat and came out of the locker room and scored eleven straight points. The Celtics came back and went ahead of us by seven. Then with some great defense we ran off a twenty to six surge. The final score was 100-95. The Bullets had beaten the Celtics in the first game of the semi-finals, and had done it in the Boston Garden.

The kid felt a little bit taller that night.

As I said, the Bullets performance at the Capital Centre that season tied a record. We knew, and the Celtics knew, that beating us at home was going to be a tall mountain to climb. The Celtics weren't able to climb that mountain. The Bullets won the series in six games. The champions were dethroned.

I felt that I had arrived as a coach in professional basketball. Our team had demonstrated that important, yet elusive, quality of a great team. I was very proud of them—but perhaps a bit too overconfident.

A couple of remarks made by Celtics players after the series have stayed with me.

"If there was one thing that surprised me," Paul Silas said, "it was that they didn't crack. I thought we could always fight back but when we did they kept their poise. That's the mark of a great team."

I thought that was a fine compliment to our team. John Havlicek made the other comment. "Playing them," he said, "is like looking in the mirror." His words touched me where I live. John understood. Being one of the greatest of the great Celtics, he would.

When I became head coach of the Bullets my goal had been to have the team achieve a kind of Celtics atmosphere. That's what Bill Sharman had done with the Lakers, and I believe that I helped him do that. I wanted to repeat that feeling with the Bullets.

Maybe I can explain this best if I talk about it in terms of cooking. I will give you now, my not so secret recipe for the one and only Celtics Pride Bread:

First, prepare a good mix of disciplined team goals. Add a strong dash of individual drive and flexibility. Stir this well so that each player know what his role is. All of this must be seasoned with a large pinch of unselfishness and understanding. This mixture will not rise unless key ingredients of scrap and hustle are included. The cook will know if his measurements are right because the mixture should create an aroma of mutual respect.

I wanted to use the same recipe with the Bullets. When the Celtics series was over I thought the bread could come out of the oven in the finals against San Francisco.

The cook was wrong. The bread got burned. So did the cook. The Golden State Warriors beat the Bullets four straight. Yep—they swept us.

In the closing minutes of the second game something happened that seemed insignificant at the time. It was only a brief moment on television, but its impact was going to rock my life.

We were behind by two points when we called a timeout. When the team came to the bench and gathered around me I said, "Run play C." This was a basic play run off a pick, a bread and butter play that the team could do in their sleep.

Bernie Bickerstaff, my assistant said, "Should I diagram it?"

I said, "Sure, go ahead." I thought diagramming the play would give the players some needed calm seconds in the bedlam.

The television camera was zeroed in on our timeout. What people saw on their sets was a team in big trouble and Coach Jones standing silently while the players huddled around a blackboard and the assistant coach diagrammed a play for them. For some reason, the local sportscaster, an ex pro-football player, made some comments about this development. He said he was surprised to see a new play being diagrammed at this point. All over the country people watched in amazement as the Bullets' assistant coach made up a play on the sideline with the game in the balance and the head coach not knowing what to do. The sportscaster let the fans know that would never have happened in a football game.

We lost the game by one point.

A thunderstorm of criticism exploded on my head. "Jones is a joke as a coach"

"He does nothing"

"His assistants run the team"

"He's unprofessional"

"Jones is unprepared for the game"

"His practices are meaningless, his team gets nothing from them."

The Washington papers, the *Post* and the *Star*, had expected the Bullets to become the champions. So did the fans. The papers began to hammer away at me. Of course, the fans were disappointed and unhappy.

The day after our loss in the second game, the sportscaster was in the Bullets office when I arrived. Bernie was diagramming and explaining the same play on a blackboard for him. I watched them for a couple of minutes, smiled and then went into my office.

The sportscaster never did explain the situation to his television audience.

The injuries to Phil Chenier and Kevin Porter didn't get better. Our backcourt was really struggling. Two more games and it was over. In each one of the four games, San Francisco, which had the momentum from the first game victory, overcame big leads to win in the final minute or so. Sometimes in the last few seconds we ran out of gas. We lost two of the games by one point. Rick Barry, the Warriors great all star, averaged over thirty points a game and played a tireless full court game that wore down our forwards.

Too often life seems to follow the "it never rains but it pours" rule. In the fourth game our scrappy guard, Mike Riordan, came off the bench and ended up in a fight with Rick Barry. After the game when the San Francisco team was celebrating their victory in their locker room, Barry, I guess, was not quite content with just the victory so he decided to tell the world that he was sure that K.C. Jones put Riordan into the game to start a fight with him so that San Francisco would lose their big scorer. He said this was typical of the kind of basketball that Jones taught. This nonsense was piled on top of everything else that was happening with me in the media. Now, if you read the sports pages and watched television, you could take your pick: I was a stupid coach who didn't know what to do during a game or I was a coach who taught dirty playing.

The sweep by San Francisco seemed to sweep away any confidence that general manager Bob Ferry had in me. From that point on our relationship became strained. I knew how disappointed Abe Pollin was, but he defended me with the press and stuck by me in every way. I believe he held this attitude with any conversations he had with Bob Ferry about me and the team.

It's the general manager's job to do what's best for the team. We lost in two finals, and lost four in a row. It seemed to leave me out on the end of a limb with Ferry. Sometimes I wondered how long the limb was going to hold me.

We spent the summer at basketball camps in New England. Even with busy days surrounded by eager youngsters the loss to San Francisco was like a blister on my heel, but no more than that. The loss was one of those things. We'd be a better team next year.

I still have questions about the business of the television scene with Bernie Bickerstaff diagramming the play. The Washington papers didn't let it go. Other sportswriters around the country played with it occasionally. As the media stayed with it, so did the fans. People in New England mentioned it, kiddingly or otherwise. I knew I had a problem with the media but I didn't know what to do about it. I was beginning to learn one of the most important lessons that people in public life can learn, and professional athletics in this country must be as public as life can be. It's a lesson every coach must learn—the media is part of the territory that goes with the job. It's a necessity, like having air in the basketball. At times what you say or do with the media can be as important as any coaching decision you make. I think for coaches this starts right at the bottom—even a Little League coach isn't going to have much of a future if the local newspaper starts banging away at him.

Pro sports is an entertainment business. The players are performers, the coach is the director. As a coach you either have charisma or you don't. You can carry a bag around with you and pull out all your goodies that tell people how terrific you are and all the great things you've done. You can play the Napoleon game with the players and the press so that you get more recognition than the players. All that stuff is foolishness and doesn't matter because the media makes or breaks you. I learned to deal with the media in an honest, on the level way. I've learned now that part of my job is to help the media people do their job.

When David Dupree, the sportswriter for *USA Today*, was working out with the team, he told Larry Bird that he was doing it because he wanted to understand what the players go through, what their job really is like. Larry, as usual, put his fingers right on the pulse when he said that he himself should try to better understand what the sportswriters' job is like. I noticed this year that Larry handled the media like a Ronald Reagan or a Jack Kennedy. It's not sacrilegious to speak of Larry that way. Don't be misled by his down-home Indiana style. Larry is one of the most perceptive people I have ever met in my life.

I wish I had learned as fast as Larry that the media can grind you into bits if you don't pay attention. In my days with the Bullets I had a problem with all that, and I'm going to try and make sure I won't have that problem again. I don't intend to be a showboat. I don't have an untapped reservoir of charisma. My only color is in my skin. I don't think I fit the media image of a professional basketball coach. I don't like to make a lot of noise and march up and down the sidelines screaming and hollering. Don't get me wrong, sometimes I raise my voice at halftime or after some game when we've played ugly. I say some things to the referees that I wouldn't want printed in this book or any book, but I am not a drill sergeant and I can't be. I'm like they say —laidback. I suppose you could say that the quiet kid has become a quiet man. The only sound I really like to have come out of my mouth in public is music. I'll sing anywhere, anytime, and I love it, but I understand now that dealing with the media and being as cooperative and fair as you can is part of a coach's job. I want to do it as well as I do the rest of my job. With the Bullets my only concern was coaching—that was a mistake.

The effort with the media does make a difference. If you let them know in a quiet way the strategy behind some of your moves, they'll try hard to be fair. Here's an example: In the 1974–1975 playoffs with the Bullets we had a grouchy, dog eat dog seven game series with Buffalo. After the last game we had a very short break before we played the Celtics. I squeezed in a quick practice session at the Capital Centre before we left for Boston. I wanted to show the players some defensive moves so they could concentrate on them and practice them in their minds on the way to Boston. The local media referred to this workout as, "a meaningless practice," and said that I would have the players "worn out before they even got to play the mighty Celtics."

Now, here we are in the 1985–1986 season—I was very concerned about the team after the fifth game loss in Houston. Some defensive and offensive moves needed to be worked on right away. None of us wanted this series to go to seven games. There were some changes that would help prevent that and the team and I needed to discuss these changes. Despite the weather and the trip from Houston, when we got back to Boston we went right from the airport to the Garden for a hard practice session. The media seemed to understand what I was trying to do. There was no criticism. Somebody told me that a couple of New England writers wrote that they thought it was a smart idea.

Has the media changed? No, I have.

The 1975–1976 season wasn't an easy one for anyone in the Jones family. In my first two years the Bullets had finished first in our division. In 75–76 we came in second. I won't go into a lengthy recital of our injury list. I'll simply say it was longer than a coach expects. We dropped down from our sixty wins of the previous year to forty-eight victories. That's not a shabby record. In fact, I remember being proud to read in a Boston paper back then that the Bullets had more wins in the three seasons that I had been with them than any other team in the NBA. We had won 155 games in three years. I wish that I had read that in a Washington newspaper.

Of course the problem was that we had not won the championship. I had been hoping that the 75–76 team would really make its mark and improve on the year before.

As I look back on that season, I think the Bullets' coach might have spent a little too much time looking over his shoulder. From the beginning of the early practice season it was clear that my relationship with Bob Ferry was not going to improve. When the season started I found myself in his office too often explaining why I didn't play so and so or did play so and so or did or didn't give a player more or less minutes in a particular situation. We all worked very hard that year. The pressures built up—something that happens to a lesser or greater degree with every season. I was hoping that we'd get everybody healthy for the playoffs and we'd redeem ourselves, that we'd surprise the sportswriters and put rings on our fingers.

The Bullets played their poorest basketball in three years in our play-off series against Cleveland. We were terrible. We lost in seven games. Bill Fitch was the Cleveland coach then. He did a great job with that team that year. If for some strange reason you're not a basketball fan and you're reading this book, I should tell you that you will meet Bill Fitch again as our paths cross.

Cleveland then took the Celtics to a tough seven games. The Celtics outlasted them and won the Championship that year. The way the Washington press and some of our fans saw it, the Bullets, and especially their coach, had left a string of disappointments behind them as they ended the season.

Mercy!

A week after the playoffs were over, a reporter for the *Washington Star* wrote a column that ripped me apart both as a coach and as a person. It was so personal that I decided to do something I had never done before, I picked up the phone and called the reporter. I asked him if the point of his column was to get me fired. I said that some of the things he wrote were not accurate or true, and I said I thought he should have talked with somebody in the organization before putting that kind of material in print. He said he had talked with somebody in the organization. When I asked him who, he said he had spoken on the telephone with a member of the management.

I'm not sure what I did after I hung up. I think I sat and stared at the wall for a few minutes hoping it wasn't true that the misinformation in that column had come from someone in our organization.

That day a friend of mine told me he had overheard a conversation with the reporter and a member of the Bullets' management at a prize fight. He told me the words spoken about me were hardly favorable. He hesitated to repeat the conversation, but after reading the newspaper article, he said he felt obligated to tell me.

Whether the piece was fabricated from an "unnamed source" based on the alleged conversation, I'll never know. All I do know is that it hurt both ways, and I could feel my own defensive hackles beginning to rise.

Later, the general manager called me into his office to offer his input on the article. He explained what he felt were the reasons for the negative report and somehow made me feel better about it. It was really a matter of accepting the medicine. He was fair with me and that helped, somewhat, to ease the pain of the writing that began to show more clearly on the wall.

After the playoffs Abe Pollin asked me to meet him early in the morning for coffee and donuts. We got together in his office about eight o'clock. Abe and I had become close. I could tell he was terribly uncomfortable. I had sensed that he was laboring over what to do about me since the end of the season and the article in the *Star*. I was confident that I could continue to give him a good coaching performance, but we hadn't won an NBA ring and the combined pressures of the newspapers, the fans, and his general manager must have been really intense. He was laboring as he spoke but the message was clear. The Bullets were letting me go.

I thought my first reaction to being fired was relief. It was over.

Abe Pollin didn't like firing me. I was sure of that then and I'm sure of it now. He told the press later that it really hurt and I believe him. He was a class guy toward me in every way. My contract was up at that time. Abe really had no further obligations to me, but he paid me for another year. He also kept Bernie Bickerstaff—I was very happy for that. I like Abe Pollin. He's as fair a man as any I've ever met.

I remember the rest of that day as though it just happened.

I was scheduled to play in a golf tournament that morning. I left Abe's office and went to the golf course and played. I don't think I said three words. Nobody there knew that I'd been fired. After the golf there was a charity event that I had promised to attend. I went through the motions there. Finally, I ran out of things to do—there was nothing else to do but go home and I didn't want to. Beverly was waiting up. I didn't say much. She told me that all that day the press had been trying to find me. They wanted to know my reaction. What was I going to say? "I've got the best record of anybody in the NBA in the last three years and now I'm out of a job."

No, there was nothing to say. I don't think I could have put three consecutive sentences together that day anyway. I had been told by a man I respected that I had failed in my career. Firing me gave that message to my family, to my friends and to the sports world.

That's as total as rejection can get. I had been a public winner—now I was a public loser. My earlier perception of my feeling was very wrong. It was not relief that I was feeling. I was shattered.

In my time with the Bullets I had come to believe that I had one definite skill—I knew how to coach basketball. I had complete confidence in that ability. I understood I had lots to learn in the business world but in the world of professional basketball, I could be the teacher. I knew I was a very good teacher. I had worked as hard as I could to learn every aspect of the game. I had given everything to basketball.

Chapter Thirteen

After being fired by the Bullets as a coach I began to fall apart as a man. I was embarrassed in front of my wife and kids. It was uncomfortable sitting around the house. I had never been that kind of a homebody. Many of the good times we had as a family were on trips and outings. I was used to being on the move. My schedule had always been wrapped around a basketball with the golf course as a place for relaxation.

I made some phone calls about basketball jobs. Never mind a job. I couldn't even find any encouragement. Nobody even called me back.

I spent more and more time at the golf course. As that time increased, so did my drinking.

I had never been much of a drinker. Some of that was Bill Russell's influence. He always said drinking was a loser's habit. He used to take one drink a year—when we won a championship. Sometimes that drink was a bottle of champagne. But that was it for him for the year. Knowing Russell I'm sure that if we hadn't won a title he'd wait until we did to have that drink. I enjoyed a couple of cold beers once in awhile or a glass of white wine but that was it.

Now it was different. I drank more. I was getting into the loser's habit.

Life had made a hard run at me but it shouldn't have knocked me over. As long as I've been black I've known that's the way things could be. Life and basketball are not that different. When the other team starts to swamp you, you call time-out, regroup and go back out and play your game.

I wasn't able to regroup. One thing that would have made a big difference was a job offer, but there weren't any. Not a single one.

'll try not to make excuses, but back then there weren't very many blacks in professional sports management. It seemed that if you were black and wanted to reach the upper levels, you would have to produce ten times better than your peers. I began rationalizing that as a black coach who had just been fired, my chances were slim to none to get rehired.

Nobody was interested in hiring me. At least that's the impression I got when I couldn't get anybody to answer my calls or my letters.

Blacks are accepted in any sport now as players—except perhaps polo. Now that I think of it, I'll have to talk to Russell about taking up polo. It would be fun to watch him galloping around on one of those little polo ponies. You know what? If I know Russell he'd end up being the first black king of the polo players.

My color wasn't the only reason that I wasn't getting any job offers from the pros. I truly believe that everything that had been printed and said about the head coach standing by while the assistant chalked X's and O's on the board had done me considerable damage. I knew I would have to chase the jobs that opened up. I hoped that a top notch college would respect my background and my record and want me to be part of their program on a long term basis, or that a pro franchise that was dragging would look to me to take a loser and turn it around. I was sure I could do that.

As the months went by and the silence grew, I became less and less sure of anything except that having some drinks and sitting around a bar with some happy-go-lucky people kept me from thinking that my basketball coaching career had fallen flat on its face, that I might not have a chance to rebound. I began to doubt my ability to support my family. I kept waiting for basketball to remember me.

It was a long wait. I had gone almost a year without getting an answer from any of the people I had contacted. I had written to colleges around the country. I couldn't even get an interview. I had called and written to teams in the NBA. The only response I had received was from the Chicago Bulls who flew me out to Chicago for an interview, but they decided to stay in-house and hire Ed Badger, now a scout with the Celtics.

My basketball life had been a series of doors opening, each one giving me an opportunity to learn more and to support my family. As time went on it seemed that all doors were closed to me. Basketball had deserted me, and if basketball didn't want me, who would?

After all my talk about blacks not getting many chances at executive positions in professional sports, I suppose it's ironic for me to tell you now that when basketball did remember me and the phone finally rang, a black executive named Wayne Embry was on the other end.

Wayne ended his basketball playing career with us on the Celtics after some outstanding years playing for Cincinnati. As great as those Cincinnati days were though, they didn't include a championship ring. Wayne wanted a ring. Everyone who ever played a pro sport does or should. If they don't want one, I don't want them on my team.

Wayne is a very astute individual. After years of hard work on the court with Cincinnati he gave the team the option of trading him to the Celtics or retiring him. How did Wayne know the Celtics could use him? I guess that's his secret. Cincinnati knew that Wayne meant to quit if he couldn't get to spend his last years in Boston so they traded him for a draft choice.

Wayne accomplished his goal. He wears a championship ring that he earned with the 1967–1968 Celtics.

Wayne Embry has just recently been made general manager of the Cleveland Cavaliers. He hired Lenny Wilkens to be his coach. I guess that executive combination makes hash out of my comments about blacks not getting a second chance for those kind of jobs. That's why I'm not planning to be a social philosopher when my basketball days are over.

In the middle of the 1976–1977 season the Milwaukee Bucks had an explosion at the top. Larry Costello, the main man in Milwaukee, was let go. Wayne Embry moved Don Nelson, his pal from Celtics days, from his job as assistant coach to head coach. Nelson called me to ask if I would be interested in the assistant coach's job in Milwaukee. I must have said yes just as fast as Bernie Bickerstaff did years before out in San Diego.

When I arrived in Milwaukee it was a bitter cold January day. Wayne, Nellie, and owner Jim Fitzgerald and I talked and I signed a contract. Somebody pointed at the line and I signed it. I figured I was in no position to be reading the fine print in a contract. The timing was good because the Jones family was just about to run out of Abe Pollin's kindness.

Later that day Nellie drove me around the Milwaukee area and showed me some areas that he thought would be good places for the family to settle. Later in the evening Wayne, his wife, Terry, and I spent some more time talking about houses and schools. Terry was Beverly's friend and I knew she could be helpful.

Terry Embry is a lady with a great deal of substance. She graduated from college and went on to earn a master's degree, but her talents are much more than academic. Wayne and Terry stayed in Boston for a few years after Wayne retired from the Celtics. Terry went to work for the Boston Redevelopment Authority. It didn't take long for her to rise to the top there, as she has in a number of other ventures. In this case she was responsible for the South End project, an area of Boston with more than its share of problems. The job involved complicated urban renewal decisions that created sensitive neighborhood racial waves. People said that watching Terry handle some of the wild and wooly white and black radicals of the 60's was a real treat. Terry Embry is nobody's pushover.

Somewhere in the Chestnut Hill area just outside of Boston there is a woman who knows how tough Terry can be. She discovered this one day in Bloomingdale's department store out there. Terry had just bought an ironing board. The lady, who was white, cruised over to the black lady with the ironing board and asked her sweetly how much she charged to do shirts. Terry's comments might have taught the lady some words she had never heard before.

I hoped that having the Embrys in Milwaukee would make the move from Maryland easier for Beverly and the kids. They needed all the help they could get at that time because I was still floundering. That there was no head coaching job for me anywhere in the country was a fact that kept my ears pushed way down. In the end, however, we decided it would be best if the family stayed in Maryland and moved to Milwaukee at the end of the school year.

Don Nelson had retired from the Celtics the previous year. This was his first coaching job. He had been an assistant for the first half of the season. Now he and the Milwaukee players were trying to get used to the idea of him as head coach. I figured my job was to make things go as smoothly as possible for the new coach. Nellie had been a heady player with the Celtics and I expected him to be that kind of a coach.

The Milwaukee ownership had changed coach and general manager because the team was struggling. The struggle continued for the rest of the year. It's a tough, tough job for a coach to take over a basketball team in the middle of a season. Don Nelson's coaching philosophy was quite different than Larry Costello's had been.

You might wonder what my reaction and approach to this situation were. I had lived the game all my adult life. I had more head coaching experience than Nellie had. What about my philosophy and system? That was on the shelf. Nobody had to explain that to me. An assistant coach is an arm or a hand or sometimes a little finger of the head coach. There can't be two systems or approaches. The head coach lives and dies with the team's success and the assistant must support the coach in everything he says and does. Jimmy Rodgers and Chris Ford give me that and that's what I gave Don Nelson. I believed his victories would be our victories. However, they were awfully hard to come by. At the season's end we'd only had thirty of them.

Sometime in March I thought I sensed a coolness coming from Don Nelson. I wasn't certain that I was reading it right. My antenna were not completely operational at the time. I still felt as though I was in a deep hole. I was convinced that when basketball fans looked at me they saw a man who had been fired in Washington. My Milwaukee days were a combination of working at basketball and in my spare time sipping beer. Milwaukee is a friendly town and a great sports city. There are lots of folks to sit and chat with. I got to know a lot of them.

It's strange when I look back at some of those years. I expect that I seemed pleasant and happy. I've never been a hard person to get along with. What the public was seeing, of course, wasn't what was going on inside. I had a small apartment downtown but where I was really living was down in the dumps. Somewhere inside me— where ever it is that Mr. Mood lives—things were as dark as my skin. The Bullets had been named right. My confidence and my self-esteem were both shot. Maybe sitting in a bar when I wasn't working at basketball was my way to get a handle on my depression or to kid myself about it. Let me tell you clearly—it doesn't work. I tell you that at no charge. It cost me a lot to learn it.

There was a little bar in Milwaukee owned by a fellow who was a good friend to the team. I walked in there at cocktail hour a couple of nights after the season ended. Nellie, Wayne and Rick Sund, the director of player personnel, were sitting in a corner. Since I seldom saw that threesome out socially, it seemed odd to see the three of them sitting there together. I walked over and had a drink with them. I thought Rick looked at me a bit peculiarly. Some friends of mine called to me from across the room and I went over to them. When I left later I was still puzzled by something I couldn't pinpoint.

Sally's restaurant was another favorite spot for me. I went in there later in the evening to eat. The same threesome were in there having dinner. I thought it was strange that they hadn't asked me to join them. I ate dinner, went home and hit the sack.

About seven-thirty in the morning Nellie called. He wanted to talk to me. A couple of minutes later the doorbell rang. It was Nellie with coffee and donuts. While I was struggling into my jeans, Nellie sipped some coffee. Without any change of expression, in a tone of voice that was just as though he were talking about the weather, he said, "K.C. I'm releasing you."

He kept on talking but I couldn't hear what he said. There was a great, loud buzzing in my ears. I do remember asking him if I should be at the college draft meeting which was the next day. Nellie shrugged and left. He was a head coach. He had things to do. I knew about that. I had just learned exactly what an assistant's life could be like.

The next day I went to the draft meeting. There were bright lights and cameras. It all seemed to hurt my eyes and my head. After a few minutes, I left. I went around town, paid up my bills and went back to Maryland. On the trip back I thought about my few months in Milwaukee, and I realized that I really hadn't done the best job as assistant coach for Nellie. The better part of my head was still reeling from the whole Washington incident. I just couldn't get my old focus back.

Coming home that night to our house in Maryland I had the same feeling that I had when I trudged back to our little shack down in Texas when the teacher sent me home from school because I couldn't read or write. I was ashamed of myself.

Beverly was cheery and helpful as always. She never complained about things. She spoke encouraging words. I didn't even hear them. I think she always felt that somehow the Lord would provide. The way I was handling things for my family it looked as though He was going to have to.

I said the Bullets firing had devastated me. I think that's accurate. Getting fired in Milwaukee almost destroyed me. I had been dropped as a head coach and learned that I couldn't get another chance to do that. Now the basketball world knew that I couldn't keep an assistant coach's job. My basketball life had hit the bottom. What would I do? What could I do? I believed I could coach winning basketball. I had proved it. Now it didn't make any difference and the belief was fading fast.

Old friends called and tried to help. Bill Russell invited me to spend some time with him on the West Coast. I hung around out there for a little while. Later he said I was as quiet then as I had been during our first months together at USF.

Willie Naulls had me stay with him. He tried to pep me up just like Russell had. They both worked hard at livening me up, but I was just too low down to reach. I couldn't talk and I felt about three feet tall.

My everlasting friends, Steve Curly and his wife Bryna, who were always kind to Beverly and me, tried to help. Their home is in Massachusetts, we were in Maryland but that didn't really mean anything to them. Friendship could leap mountains and they would be willing to try that to help, but the person they wanted to help couldn't help himself.

I felt as though a great weight was pressing me down. The one thing in my life that I was sure of, the game, and the only business that I understood like a fish understands the water, had dried up on me.

There were plenty of people to have a drink with or sing a song with, but that wasn't the world I wanted. I was going to have to deal with the fact that the world I wanted didn't want me.

Every year at the summer basketball camps I had to make a little speech to the kids. It was always agony. I have never felt that I could grab the right words in a speech. That year it was worse than ever. I figured some of those kids had to be thinking that here is a guy talking to us about basketball who can't hold a job in basketball. It's amazing what you project when you're down. That's where I was. I was embarrassed in front of those kids, and worse than that I was embarrassed in front of my own kids.

Chapter Fourteen

Fortunately for me the ball is round and the court is flat. They play the game just about everywhere. Richmond, Virginia is one of the places they play. Richmond was joining a new pro-basketball minor league. It's where the players who haven't made the grade in the NBA and are working to climb up that tall ladder go. This is also true of the coaches. I suppose it was the right place for me at the time. The way my career was going, it seemed I would have to take whatever was available.

Suddenly, before I even got started in Richmond, one of my dearest friends reached out his hand to me and opened a very large door. Satch Sanders was made head coach of the Celtics. Satch had been assistant to Tommy Heinsohn who had been let go mid-season after a brilliant record. Now Satch called and asked me to be his assistant. Satch's offer was like throwing a drowning man a life raft. Being the pure man that he is, he never mentioned it. I'm sure Satch knew the shape I was in.

Heinie had won five division titles and two NBA championships with the Celts. He'd run the team for eight or nine years and in my opinion was a great coach. Heinie was a hard driving, noisy, colorful coach. Sometimes his theatrics at courtside made people forget that this is a brilliant man. He's a guy who will succeed at anything in life. He felt then that his style was out of sync with the times. When I got to Boston and looked and listened in the locker room, it was clear to me that the problem hadn't been Heinie. The fact is, some of the players' attitudes at that time were not in the Celtic's tradition.

Satch told me that that year at the team's traditional Christmas party at the Garden— a party that over the years everybody had looked forward to—only John Havlicek and Jo Jo White and their families showed up. Wives and players and kids loved it. It was a time that reminded us all that the Celtics were a family. Satch said it was a sad thing to watch Red go around and pick up all the gifts he'd gotten for kids and wives who hadn't come. Some sort of dissatisfaction had developed and it would take a lot to bring it back.

If you watch the NBA on television now, you can hear Heinie talk about the game and you will be getting an excellent coaching lesson from a fellow who knows the game inside out. Some people criticized him for coming down hard on Ralph Sampson when he punched up Jerry Sichting and Dennis Johnson in our fifth game with Houston this past year's playoffs. They thought Heinie was allowing a little Celtics' favoritism to spill over. No way. If one of our players had done that, it would be very hard to defend and Heinie would have responded appropriately—and there have been times when some of us have thought Heinie was calling things the other way. Those of us who know Heinie understand that he calls them as he sees them. That's the way he's been all his life. Red is the only person who has ever made Heinie look at his toes—but most of us who played for Red have done that. Believe me, if Heinie's doing a Celtic game and the players or the coach are out of order, he'll let the viewers know about that too because he's an on the level guy.

The Celtics fans are extremely fortunate with their television coverage these days. All year long they get Bob Cousy and his partner, Gil Santos. Even if you don't like the Celtics, you've got to like the job Cous and Gil do. They're both pros at their job. Cous was a genius on the court and he's been just as brainy after he left the game. The way Bob Cousy has conducted himself through life has made him one of the most respected men I know.

I don't think Heinsohn or Cousy will ever leave the New England area. They've become institutions—like their college. Holy Cross must be very proud of those two guys.

Speaking of being proud of somebody that's become an institution brings to mind the one and only, never a duplicate—although they have contests to pick sound-a-likes—Johnny Most. Johnny has covered the Celtics on radio for centuries. If you cut him the guy would bleed Celtic Green. He lives for the team. I've loved him since I was black, and I've always trusted the fact that he's been in my corner. A friend of John's and later a very close friend of mine, flugle horn master Emil

Haddad of Worcester, first talked me into singing in public. It happened years ago—right around the time when I was a rookie—in a place called the Meadows in Framingham, now the sight of commercial development near Shopper's World. The Meadows was reputedly owned by the great singer-band leader, Vaughn Monroe.

Emil told the orchestra I had a great set of pipes. Then he pushed me up to sing. I loved it. No shyness, the words were right there on my tongue for me. I've been doing it ever since. I still sing with Emil's band when I'm in Worcester.

For those of us on the Celtics, Johnny Most is part of our life and belongs in the Hall of Fame with the team. There are a lot of funny stories about Johnny but I'd like to keep his friendship—so I won't tell them. Well, maybe just one crack that Heinie used to make. He said the fans always got a double header when they listened to Johnny do a game. There was the game on the court and the game Johnny was announcing. Still, it's a fact that lots of fans keep a radio on while they watch us on TV.

Celtics fans get some extra treats from the media crews these days. We've had some terrific people cover the team.

I meet fans who have never been in the Garden but tell me they feel as though they've been right by my side in our games. That's a genuine compliment to the print and electronic sports media in the Boston area and beyond.

Returning to the Boston area was part pleasure, part pain for me. I was a guy who had coached a team that beat a fine Celtics team and then lost the finals by some eyelashes and got fired. Then got dumped from an assistant coach's job in Milwaukee. I'm sure you've all got the message by now—I just wasn't proud of myself.

The pleasure was the chance to renew many old friendships with people like Steve and Bryna Curley and Hy Horwitz and his family.

Hy befriended the Celtics when I was a player, and many a day between practice sessions and training camp, the whole team would be invited to lunch at Hy and Sylvia Horwitz' home in Waban, MA. I can still see the whole troop of giant men draped over this chair or that table, chowing down. Jim Hadnot, a really big fellow, would eat off the top of the refrigerator. Sylvia made sure everybody's plate was always full.

Dave and Nancy Horwitz, who were then in high school, enjoyed chatting with the players. As time went by, we became close personal friends. The Horwitz family were great fans, too. Hy and Sylvia have passed on, but Dave and his family remain very close.

To be back with the Celtics was the greatest thing that could have happened to me, but I still had a chip on my shoulder to prove myself. I wished I were coming back in better shape. Obviously Red still had confidence in me or he never would have approved Satch bringing me back. I wanted to please Red. I suppose I have been wanting to please him from the day I first walked into the Celtics' training camp. I know it's possible to get carried away with this kind of thinking, but maybe he's a bit of a father-figure to me.

I can tell by Red's expressions and his actions what he's thinking. When I was a player I used to do an imitation of him that would have the guys roaring. I can do Red's walk, talk, his hands with the cigar — the whole bit. One day in the locker room I was not getting the roaring response I usually got from the other players. I turned around and there was Red, leaning against the doorway, watching me. Ouch!

In the last three years, seeing Red accepting those two NBA Championship trophies has been one of the delights of my life.

Well, let's get back to moving to Boston. This time we didn't wait until school was over. We found a house in Andover, a town about twenty miles north of Boston and settled in. I still wasn't doing the kind of job I should have been on the home front. My wife never complained. She just continued being a great mother. Her brother Herbie came home from Vietnam and stayed with us. Her other brother, David, got out of the service and stayed for awhile too. I should have been feeling a great sense of family both at home and with the Celtics. I was surrounded with people who cared about me, but I couldn't see them. I seemed to be drifting on a lonely sea.

That 1977–1978 Celtics team was in a similar shape to my own.

Satch had inherited the most serious mess the Boston Celtics had ever been in. Thank goodness he didn't know that the next year would be even worse. Of any coaching job I've ever heard of, Satch had the wrong job at the wrong time, and of any coach I've ever seen, Satch worked the hardest. Nobody could have made that team play pretty. You know by now that I believe that chemistry is more important than X's and O's. The team's grade in chemistry at that time was a failing one, and no coach could have reached them. Celtics Pride seemed to have been forgotten. Yet strangely two members of that team, in fact the heart of the good years of that team under Heinie, were still there. Both great stars who were the essence of Celtics Pride, John Havlicek and Dave Cowens would do whatever was necessary to win. They were classic unselfish Celtics players.

Dave Cowens played basketball with his head and his body and his heart. If the team didn't win—it broke his heart. Some people called him the highest jumping white man that ever played basketball. I always thought he was such a terrific rebounder because he had so much desire. I believe the frustration of the next couple of crazy years with the Celtics, combined with injuries that came from playing as hard as he could every minute, caused Dave to leave the game sooner than he should have.

John Havlicek had an awesome career—one of the greatest in the history of American professional sports. He was mentally and physically tough. He took great care of his body.

Scott Wedman is just like him in many ways—a lean and hungry greyhound.

John studied and learned every aspect of the game. I never saw another player grow steadily into greatness as he did.

Larry Bird was a great player from his first day in the NBA. John Havlicek became a great player. He understood that to move without the ball on the offense breaks down the defense. It's so simple yet so hard for so many players to learn.

When you're moving you are one hundred times harder to defend. You know what moves you're going to make. The defender doesn't—unless he's a mind reader. Young players must work at that. No, I don't mean mind reading. I mean they must work at moving without the ball when they're on offense on a basketball court. I think that young players on a team that doesn't have alert, unselfish veteran players get discouraged. A youngster tries his hardest moving on the court and nothing happens. No one passes the ball to him. He finally says, "The heck with this. I'm working my butt off and I never touch the ball." Or, if he gets the pass, he doesn't have the confidence to do something with the ball.

I remember Russell's crack about Sam Jones as a rookie. He called Sam "Right Back" because when Sam began in the NBA his confidence level was low and the minute you gave him the ball you got it Right Back. Sam learned—oh boy, did he. What a player he was. Don't be a "right back" player. A confident player is a thinking player. After the key ingredient of hustle, the key to successful basketball is don't panic—think.

If there was ever a thinking basketball player and a thinking man, it is Satch Sanders. He is also a very funny man with a philosopher's sense of humor who has enough confidence to laugh at himself.

Satch stories, as you know, are plentiful. One of the things that I think is terrific about the stories is that most of them come from him.

Another one of my favorites is the story about Satch and Russell driving home from New York. We had played the Knicks in New York and for some reason or other Russ had his big new Cadillac in the city. He and Satch were driving back to Boston after the game. Russ was exhausted so it was decided that Satch would drive when they got out of the city. They stopped for a minute and Russ explained the cruise control on the car to Satch.

Did Satch understand?

"Put the car at 60, 70, 80, whatever, set the thing and we'll cruise to Boston. Just stay awake and steer. O.K.?"

"O.K."

Russ climbed in the back and went to sleep. All 6'9" or 10" of him.

Remember, Satch is telling this story.

At about one-thirty, two o'clock in the morning, the Caddy is moving at a set seventy miles an hour, whistling along the Connecticut Turnpike. Satch spots a toll booth ahead. Now his hands are flying all over and under the dash board.

He shows you.

Trying to figure out how to turn the cruise control off. Here comes the toll booth. The guy in the booth's eyes are wide, wide open. His mouth is just the same.

Here comes the Caddy at seventy miles an hour with Satch at the controls, his eyes and mouth just as wide as the guy in the booth. The Caddy goes right through the toll booth at the same seventy miles an hour.

Satch is now yelling and hollering at the car. Russell wakes up in the back seat and sits up.

"What the hell is going on?"

Satch, "Oh, nothing, nothing."

Satch says to himself, "Man, I'm glad I wasn't doing that guy's laundry that night."

That's a small part of Satch. The big part is a serious, dedicated man. Right now he is involved with The Center for the Study of Sport in Society at Northeastern University, a program that is designed for athletes of all ages to balance their education with their athletic dreams. They also help athletes get the degrees they never got and the education they didn't pay any attention to and wish they had.

I hope that Satch story gave you a good chuckle because we don't have anything funny coming up in this story for quite awhile.

Satch's term as head coach was a horror story of some players with bad attitudes. We also suffered from a ton of injuries—most of them real. At one time in that first year on a West Coast trip we called a guy on the phone who lived in Seattle. He hadn't touched a basketball in over a year. We gave him a ten day contract and played him out there. He was the only big man we could recruit quickly. He played two or three games for us and we retired him. He never made it to the Garden. Wacky? Just run of the mill during that stretch.

Havlicek announced he was going to retire at the end of the season. That was a sign of the times for sure.

Red was not lying down for all of this. That'll never be his style. He was keeping an eye on a kid in Indiana, a 6'9" forward named Larry Bird. Red sent me on a scouting trip to check out Mr. Bird soon after I got back with the Celtics. When I got back from the trip I told Red that Larry Bird was the most confident athlete I had ever seen in my life—in any sport, anywhere.

Picture this—the Indiana State team is playing, I think it was Southern Methodist. Larry is being double and triple teamed every time he gets the ball. He gets away on a fast break but there are two guys hanging on him as he goes down the court. Larry fires the ball off the backboard at an angle, simultaneously zigging away from the two defenders. They think he's just thrown up a crazy shot. Larry goes right to where he knows the ball would come off the board and in the air he takes the pass he's just made to himself and dunks the ball. I had never seen anybody have the presence of mind and the self-confidence and the ability to put something like that together.

Red decided to draft Larry even though he was only a junior. If he used hardship, he could leave school and play, and could have helped the Celtics immediately. But Larry is Larry, the one and only. Naturally he stuck with his teammates at Indiana State and played out his senior year with them, finishing his college career by starring in the NCAA finals.

It seemed clear, though, that Larry wanted to be a Celtic when he graduated. That was the one bright spot in the 1978–1979 season for the Celtics.

As things with the team got uglier and uglier, Satch worked harder and harder. But nobody could achieve success in that situation. I tried to help him in any way or every way, but I was having a difficult time trying to help myself.

I kept sliding down hill. I knew it but I couldn't seem to do anything to stop it. The worse I felt about myself, the worse I acted.

I f you drive a car in a senseless way, you're a good candidate for a bad crash. One night it came to me that I was on the way to a crash with my life.

One of my children was in a school play. That's the sort of event that should be a happy family outing with everyone making an effort to support the brave one who is going to be up there on the stage. All the family would be there to say, "Hey, we're with you."

I was there all right. I'd prepared myself for the play by doing some drinking. The way I behaved must have made the kids wonder where the father they'd known had gone. I was foolish and discourteous—joking and laughing while the play was going on onstage. My child's performance was fine. Mine was awful.

At two o'clock that morning I was at home sitting at the kitchen table. I knew I was getting close to rock bottom. If I didn't stop this slide I would end up sleeping in the gutter, and my wife and kids would be in the gutter with me because I was dragging them along. I had to get away from them to save them. If I was going down I'd go down alone.

I woke up Beverly and told her I was leaving—right then. I had to do it. I hated it but it seemed to be the only possible option. I was disgracing my wife and my kids. They were wonderful people. They didn't deserve having me and my deterioration around. I had to let them have and keep their pride.

Maybe none of this makes sense now. It seemed to make awful, terrible sense then. Here I was doing the same thing my father had done. I knew how devastating that was, yet I was repeating the act. There was nothing else I could do.

I went to live with a friend, Dr. Joe Fowler, in Boxford, MA.

Afterwards when Beverly and I talked, she kept saying she was sure that it was her fault, that she had failed me. I never could make her understand that I was the one who had failed and that she and the kids paid the price for my failure with me.

Chapter Fifteen

S ome terrible things were also happening to the Celtics family. The 1977–1978 disaster was behind us. The owner, Irv Levin, told the world everything would be different this year. He was right. A couple of weeks later he traded the franchise, the whole bag, to a fellow named John Y. Brown who owned the Buffalo team. The deal was that Buffalo would become Boston and Boston would become San Diego. Some players would stay in Boston and others would go to the coast. Some good trades Red had made were completely down the drain. At that moment you had a situation where Red, the coaches, Dave Cowens and a few other players had more loyalty to the team than the owners.

Mercy!

Satch was now doomed as coach. That was clear to both of us. It became crystal clear when John Y. Brown called Satch in and told him he should start throwing chairs around and getting in some big fights with the officials to give the crowd some excitement.

"It's just show biz," he said.

Satch told him in his quiet way that that was not his style, that this was the Boston Celtics not Barnum and Bailey. He thought of himself as a coach not a clown.

Satch was gone soon. The team was barely alive. He has never had another chance to coach in the NBA. His first effort shouldn't even be counted. He can be an outstanding coach. He deserves a fair shot. I hope to see that happen in the future.

Something must be said here, something that might explain the kind of people the real Celtics are. If you attend one of our practices, you might see Red and Satch sitting with their heads together talking about everything and anything, the two of them comfortable and happy with one another. The same with Heinie and Red—still close as can be. Those fellows know they were as fair and honest with each other as they could be. They are still loyal to one another and have mutual respect. They know what hard decisions have to be made in this business.

Red made two major decisions in a row. The time just wasn't right for Heinie or Satch. Now he tried a player/coach to see if he could get the players' attention.

Dave Cowens got the job. It didn't change things. The rest of the year continued ugly. Players came and went. The owner's wife liked Bob McAdoo of the Knicks. Brown brought McAdoo to the team without talking to Red. Brown traded the draft choices Red was saving to rebuild the team and gave the Knicks some money to get McAdoo so his wife would be happy.

I guess you could say that's a man who likes to please his wife.

It drove Dave Cowens and the basketball part of the organization insane. Bob McAdoo was not the answer to the Celtics problems. Red was going to quit and join the Knicks organization which had offered him a blank check deal. Life was more confusing and chaotic than it had ever been with the Celtics. Mr. Brown was proving to be a disruptive force in the Celtics organization, which up to now had an unblemished record.

Red almost did leave. I think his wife talked him out of it, but I don't think his heart would have been complete with any other team in the league. He forced a showdown with Brown. Red won, and Brown sold his interests in the Celtics.

Brown's partner, Harry Mangurian—a good guy and a thoughtful and considerate man—took over ownership of the team. He stepped back and let Red make the deals and the basketball decisions.

The world started to change.

My world was changing too. A year and a half had passed since I had left home. I had seen turmoil all around me—nothing was in harmony. Yet, strange as it may seem, I was beginning to see and hear things more clearly. Having more time alone helped me put things in a better perspective. Renewed friendships and new relationships began to bolster my feelings. I began to go forward again.

began to bolster my feelings. I began to go forward again.

Dave Cowens gave up his coaching job at the end of Nightmare Season Two. Bill Fitch of the Cleveland Cavaliers was named head coach of the Celtics. I was retained as assistant. Somehow, this felt positive to me, like my life was taking a better direction. For the first time I could deal with just where I was and I faced the reality of never being a head coach again. I had a job, and I would be the best assistant coach in the NBA.

With Bill Fitch as my new boss, I began by looking forward to a new season and a chance to work with the new coach. It didn't take me long to determine that my role wasn't going to be as simple as I thought.

Red had brought together another strong group of players. We still had Dave Cowens. He was a rock. He'd give everything he had. He did that until there was nothing left to give.

Cedric Maxwell had gone through the bad years and had gotten better and better. He made a living around the hoop and at the foul line. He could be as good as he wanted to be.

In one of the trades that had been made during the couple of preceding years we had acquired Tiny Archibald, a wonderful, tough talent at guard. We held on to him.

We'd gotten Michael Leon Carr from Detroit. He brought with him a big heart and the fire in his belly to win, a sense of total team dedication and a great sense of humor. We got about two men in one. He would play guard or forward off the bench as a sixth man and was a number one man at driving the opposition right up the wall.

A wonderful giant of a human being named Rick Robey had joined the team the year before. He was Cowen's back up at center.

A young fellow named Gerald Henderson had come to camp a free agent and played himself onto the team as a guard with great speed, leaping ability and defensive strength.

Above all these fine players, on another level in a basketball world of his own was Mr. Larry Bird. I could go on and on about him, but I won't. I'll only say one more thing. From his first game in the league he was exactly what he'd been when I first scouted him in college—the most confident athlete I'd ever seen. He played his first minutes like a superstar and has never stopped. I recall one of Larry's first home games in the Garden. He was on the fast break with Eric Fernsten trailing, the only two players to have crossed half-court. He had the easy lay-up at the other end, but unselfish, all-knowing Larry flipped the ball back to Eric, a bench player who logged few minutes. Eric made the hoop and the Garden fans went wild, cheering Larry and Eric and the promise of great seasons to come.

What an effect he has on a team. They know he's the best and then they watch him work harder to improve his skills than anyone they've ever seen in their lives. Larry Bird is an exceptional player and just as exceptional a human being.

I've lived a lot of my life watching athletes become big stars. Celebrities. These are young men whose lives change completely—often not for the best.

Larry Bird became a star quickly and his light has grown brighter and brighter. I heard him say one day that he has an awful time going to the supermarket and getting out without being surrounded.

This little story will tell you how much being a very famous star has changed Larry.

A couple of years ago I was invited to play in a golf tournament in Terre Haute, Indiana by Jerry Manley, a friend of Larry Bird's, who, with his wife Pat and children Debbie and Mark, have become close friends of mine.

Next we traveled to French Lick to play some informal golf with Larry and Rick Robey. Larry's childhood friends were included in all the games and get-togethers. They are as important to him now as when he was growing up, and he still includes them in his life. He hasn't allowed fame and fortune to separate him from his old friendships and loyalties.

Do I need to say any more about Larry Bird?

That was the nucleus of the team Bill Fitch began his Celtics career with. Bob MacKinnon and I were the assistant coaches. Both of us were glad to be there. We were both eager to pitch in. I think both of us were disappointed that we weren't given more to do. We had more to give than was asked of us because we found out very quickly that Bill didn't want much help from anyone. Bob left and became an assistant coach with New Jersey. I became Bill's one and only assistant.

When Bill coached at Cleveland he began cultivating a friendship with Red—calling him often for basketball advice and just yakking about the game. They had coached together on a basketball trip to Japan and Red came to see Bill as the right person to turn things around for the Celtics.

The year started well. Bill had a disciplined, no nonsense approach and made it clear to everybody that he was the boss of the team in everything they did, both on and off the court—from how they had their ankles taped to how the hotel rooms were assigned. He demanded perfection from everyone.

As far as Bill and I were concerned, things got off on the right foot.

I was happy and excited, as were Red and Harry, to get a winning season in gear. We were behind Bill one-hundred percent.

Somehow, though, as the months went by our relationship got out of sync. I guess I better wrestle now with the relationship I had—or didn't have—with Bill. The camaraderie that I was used to with the coaching staff, where decisions would be discussed and opinions were respected, wasn't there. At first Bill asked me a lot of questions and appeared interested in my input. As time went on, however, that happened less and less. Before long, even in practices, I sensed he preferred me to be a silent support. This is the privilege of the head coach, of course. I had been there before so I could adjust.

However, on one or two occasions where I tried to make a point to a player in a practice situation, for whatever reason, Bill showed great displeasure.

At one point, Tiny Archibald came to see me on the court to ask about a play we were running. I tried to explain it and walk it through with him. Before I could finish, Bill called over from the other side of the court, with all the other players looking on, "Hey, Tiny, when he gets through with that stuff, come over here and I'll show you how to do it right."

OUCH!

Bill was serious and incidents like this were not isolated. Maybe it was the pressure of his first year in Boston, but he seemed to get more uptight and demanding as time went on. He told me to "Sit down and shut up" during a game situation, and my main thought was, "OK, that's what he wants—that's what I'll do." We couldn't seem to find the line of communication we needed to solve these problems.

Even though I saw Bill's methods affecting some of the less experienced players by undermining their confidence, I also saw the team improving. Our record was great. Larry and our starting five were getting rave notices. I would have to hang in there and find the line of least resistance so as not to interfere with the program.

I can't deny that anger was beginning to grow inside of me, but I tried to contain it, to read the day to day situation and go with it. I helped players quietly before or after Bill was on the practice court. I kept to myself as much as possible otherwise, and the pain was tempered by the excitement of more and more victories as the season progressed.

I became close friends with Rick Robey, the 6'11" back-up center. Rick had had a marvelous college career at Kentucky. He'd been on an NCAA Championship team there. He was a hard working bull on the court and a wonderful easy going funny man the rest of the time. In those days I think I needed some humor even more than I do now—

although it's always welcome.

Maybe some of my problems with Bill came from a long standing division among coaches that I think is foolish. There seems to be a feeling by the people who are book and student coaches that coaches who come from the playing ranks don't really know their X's and O's. Up-through-the-ranks coaches who weren't players seem to resent the players who step into top jobs. Bill is an up-through-the-ranks coach. My being an ex-player coach might have bothered him. I don't know. I do know this prejudice is silly. We should respect one another and appreciate our jobs. We're all walking a tightrope.

Who's kidding who? We're all candidates for the coaches' funny farm. All of us.

Each of us chooses his own route to that funny farm. Bill's approach and mine are different. That's nothing serious and it's not meant as a criticism. We're two very different people and so we coach differently.

Bill Fitch led a new squad with the old Celtic attitude to a dramatic turn around in the 1979–80 season. The team won sixty-one games, which equalled the number of wins in the two previous seasons. That record was the best in the NBA that year. But in the playoffs we surprised everybody by taking a nosedive against Philly.

T he next year two basketball greats entered the world of the Celtics. Robert Parish and Kevin McHale were acquired in the biggest steal Red ever made. Imagine two All Stars for one draft choice to San Francisco. Mercy! Red didn't leave his heart in San Francisco. Their heart has got to be broken every time they see those two in Celtic green.

Another important addition was Jimmy Rodgers, who was brought on board as a second assistant coach. Jimmy had been Bill's right-hand man at Cleveland and worked for him for more than a decade at different locations. I liked Jimmy immediately. He was organized and enthusiastic and, to this day, he's one of the finest assistants I know, with great potential as a future head coach or general manager.

Jimmy and Bill had a long-developed working relationship with none of the hang-ups that seemed to plague Bill and me. I tried to decipher the reasons for our differences. It's like dancing—you might get off out of sync but then you pause and hope you find the rhythm. You get your timing together and all is well.

Right here I will interrupt myself and tell you with no modesty that in my younger days I was sometimes called the best dancer in the NBA. I love to dance. Ellen, my wife now, and I have danced through most of the NBA cities and parts of Europe. We're regulars at The Last

Hurrah at the Parker House with the Winiker Band.

With Bill I could only side step and second guess. As I said before, maybe he resented player-coaches or maybe he felt threatened by my having been a former head coach. Maybe he disliked my rapport with players and fans. As long as I worked with Bill I wondered about this, and, sadly, our relationship continued to deteriorate.

What hurt was the way I was left out of strategy sessions. Once in a while a special practice would be held that I would learn about afterward. One day things would be okay and another day I'd feel the pain of being ostracized. It went up and down like that for a couple of years. It was not an easy rollercoaster to be on. I stayed with it mainly with the help of my best friend and listening post, Ellen. She'd give me encouragement, tell me to keep my head high and that someday good things would happen. She even predicted that I'd be a head coach again. I didn't believe in me as much as she did, but she had the right approach for me at the time and I'll always appreciate it. She has made a large difference in my life, which has been uphill with her wonderful support.

We won it all that second year. We beat the 76ers in seven tough games, and then went on to beat Houston 4 games to 2 for the NBA Championship.

It was such a treat to be around this team in their moment of triumph. The fans were ecstatic and the players were high on winning championship rings—their first. They had come so far, and now they had the taste of victory. Even hanging on by my fingernails, it was great to share their triumph.

I stood in the corner of the locker room with the happy noise of the players bouncing off the walls. I picked up one of the bottles of champagne and went into the trainer's room. I sat there by myself and drank some champagne. I lifted up the bottle and gave a silent toast. Celtics Pride was back.

Chapter Sixteen

Even though the Celtics had a great season and won the championship, it was an even greater year for me off the court.

Ellen and I got married.

You must be saying to yourself right now, "Who is Ellen? Where did she come from?"

Ellen comes from Connecticut originally. Our relationship really developed with the assistance of mutual friends from Waltham, Una and Rod Loynd. At this point, Ellen was the assistant director of public relations for the Sheraton Corporation and going to graduate school at Boston University. We were more similar than different and we were developing a special relationship.

I felt that my life was turning around but it was clear to me that I couldn't recapture the past. Ellen and I cared for each other and wanted to be together as a married couple. There was a problem. She is white and I continue to be black.

Our marrying was a situation that didn't make either of our families happy. I knew it was going to be a series of hurdles for both of us—especially for Ellen. I felt my mother would understand what I did. I would talk with my youngsters and hope they would accept this. Earlier, when Beverley and I first separated, I asked my children to come into the Celtics offices and I talked to them about my leaving home. I won't forget that experience either.

Luckily, Ellen has tremendous respect for family feelings. She has worked very hard to reach out to my children.

However, Ellen's own family found her marriage to me a very difficult thing to deal with. I understand that, and I hope time will heal it. Her brother, David, has been a strong rock of support for Ellen in all of this and has been a special friend to me. He is a hell of a guy.

Ellen and I flew to Santo Domingo between games to get married, accompanied by our close friends, the wonderful older couple from Waltham, who had played cupid and sort of adopted us.

If there is a book in my life, there are probably three books in Una's life. Roddy was her third husband and I always thought he watched her wondering what she was going to do next. I got to know them because she was a great Celtics fan. No, that's not right. UNA WAS A CELTICS FANATIC. She went to all the games and got to know many of the players. She wasn't hard to spot—a little lady in her seventies. I don't think she was five feet tall. She was a big Patriots fan too, and her trademark was a white mink coat and sneakers. She was Irish and proud of it. She believed that all the Celtics were Irish, one way or another. Her son, Fred, his wife, Rae, Christopher's godmother, and son Sean are still close to us.

Rick Robey was Una's special favorite. She decided that Rick had the best looking bottom in America. She had Dick Raphael, a photographer, take a shot of Rick's buns. She had Rick autograph a good sized blowup of that photograph which she hung in her house.

Rick, Quinn Buckner and Larry Bird were the "Three Musketeers" of the team at that time. They were favorites with Una and Roddy. The year of Larry Bird's first Celtic championship, a parade was held in Waltham. Una showed up in her white mink coat and her special shoes. She walked up to Larry and threw open her coat. She was wearing a t-shirt with **French Lick, Indiana** in big letters on it. Larry loved it. He picked her up and gave her a big hug to her delight. She never stopped talking about that event.

The next year she followed the team in the playoffs with the Sixers. She gave each one of the players a kiss before a big game in Philly. When we lost she said she'd never kiss anybody again. I don't think she kept her promise.

A few weeks before Una died, Quinn, Rick, and Larry made a surprise visit to her home. This meant more to her, and thus to everyone who knew her, than I can put into words.

Roddy died not long after Una—I don't think he could really live without her.

Una used to love to tell people that I was her son. She'd put her arms around me and give me a big hug. Then Una would point out Roddy and say, "That's his father." That usually got a reaction since I was the only black person in that group.

Una and Roddy insisted on flying to Santo Domingo with us to witness our wedding. We had a two day honeymoon and flew back to the team that was on its way to winning the championship.

Ellen and I miss Una and Roddy.

Actually I could take some satisfaction about being a help to the team during my years as assistant. Bill Fitch had a Marine Corps Sergeant approach. He was a tough, relentless, demanding coach. He drives his players, but never as hard as he drives himself. Sometimes a player would react negatively—very negatively—to Bill's approach to coaching. Bill had very little sympathy for players with hurt feelings. His attitude was there are only twenty-four hours in the day that we can give to basketball, so don't pout—play ball. He had a sharp tongue for those players who made mistakes. As time went on some players began to be very unhappy with the way they were treated or talked to.

Remember, in the economics of what I still like to call the game of basketball, the coach is nowhere near the top of the team's salary schedule. It's human nature for a young fellow earning nearly a million dollars a year for playing basketball to become unhappy when someone not earning as much as he does tells him that he is a dummy at the game.

There were times when I could talk quietly with a player and be of help to the team—and to the coach. If a player was down I'd try to get him up. I'd point out certain areas that a player could work on to help him become the player he wanted to be.

At one stage one of our key players came to me. No, it was not Larry—there was always mutual respect between Bill and Larry. One source for that mutual respect must have been the fact that they were the two hardest workers on the team. Anyway, a key player came and said he'd had enough jabs from Bill. He was going to announce he wanted to be traded.

We had a long talk. I pointed out how successful Bill's teams were, how the hard work and words paid off. I told him he should look around at basketball in the NBA and see what being a Celtic meant. I said Bill only wanted what every coach and player should want. Victory. Sure I said he's a hard man but he's just as hard on himself. He wants perfection from himself and his players. He believes that can be achieved by hard work and he sets the example.

The player stayed with the Celtics and I'm sure he doesn't regret it.

The year after the championship season Red worked another one of his great maneuvers. He convinced Danny Ainge to switch from professional baseball to professional basketball. Danny was reasonably confident when he joined the team in the middle of the season. As I watched him I believed that this was a young fellow who had the desire and all the tools. I could see he was a scraper in the old Celtics tradition. Only one element was missing and that was complete confidence. He was expected to become a great baseball star and he hadn't quite made it. Now he was playing for a very demanding coach who would let him know very quickly about any mistake he made. Danny would have to be brought along so that his confidence would grow to meet his talent. If that happened, he was going to be a Hall of Famer.

Sports fans, that's just what's happening. Danny is on his way to greatness.

The year was terrific until we got to the second season. We lost in the playoffs to Philly. This time it was a real nosedive because in the third game, Tiny Archibald, our play maker and team quarterback, was knocked down at mid court and separated his shoulder. That injury separated us from raising another flag up to the Garden rafters.

We had some demanding, exciting confrontations with the Sixers during those years. It was a treat to be around at those times.

However, the treats were getting fewer and fewer.

At one point during this season I made some suggestions before a game with Baltimore. I had coached the team, and I felt I could be helpful in the game plan to be used against them. Bill said thanks for the help, but no thanks and that was that. There was no doubt in my mind that Bill was just barely tolerating me being around.

I was determined to keep my mouth shut. That's never been a problem. I would be totally loyal as always and hang on as long as I could.

The world of professional basketball is a world of tension. Sitting in airports, bouncing in airplanes that scare you right into the tips of your toes. Dull hours in a hotel room, the coach watching basketball videos, trying to determine the opposition's strengths and your own team's strength against them. The players may just stare out the window for hours and then walk onto the court and try to not listen to shouting anti-Celtic crowds. Electric moments in a game, the clock ticking away like a bomb ready to explode. For the coach, always the need to win. For the player, the desire to do his job just right so that his hustle helps bring victory.

That's a recipe I could go on and on about.

The end product of all that is tension.

The tension increases or decreases at different—sometimes unexpected—times, but it's always there. It's like the foul line, it's part of the game. Let me tell you, there's plenty of tension at the foul line. That's why we endlessly shoot fouls and practice so hard running set plays and the options off them. When the tension is up near the top of your head, you can use that repetition to put yourself on cruise control.

I think one of the keys to successful professional coaching is the ability to keep that tension level down.

Sometimes, of course, it spills over. When it did with Bill and the players I could get caught in the middle.

One day out on the Coast we were running a three on three drill during practice. I was the referee. Bill was sitting high up in the stands observing. M.L. Carr, Gerald Henderson and Tiny Archibald were one team. They were defending against a fast break coming at them and didn't call out what man they were taking. Bill shouted down at them, telling them pretty clearly what he thought of their intelligence. M.L. picked up the ball and fired it off the wall near Bill. He said some very strong things to his coach—something about acting like a God looking down on the world.

I fielded the ball as M.L. kept yelling at Bill.

"Give me that ball," M.L. growled at me. I looked at Bill, looked at M.L. and flipped him the ball.

M.L. drove the ball at the wall again. He kept snapping at Bill. I fielded the ball again. Everyone stood still and quiet.

"Give me that ball," M.L. said.

I looked at Bill again. Looked at M.L. No one spoke. I flipped him the ball. He drove it at the wall again.

This time I did not field the ball.

Mercy!

Many people ask me why I never seem to lose my cool during a game. It's a very frequent question. Once in awhile I do. I boil over. When that happens it's usually directed at the referees. Sometimes the fans don't realize what a key part of the game the officiating is. The referees have a good deal to do with setting the pace and the mood of the game.

Somebody in the American Basketball Association was awfully smart when they got started because the first thing they did was steal three or four of the NBA's top referees. Whoever executed that coup understood that you can't play professional sports without professional officials. Some games are great games because the officials make the players perform at their best.

Of course, once in a while that coin has another side.

If you're human you're going to explode at the refs sometimes. They're human too and they're trying to do a job that is more complicated than two people can handle. I don't know how much refs get paid, but I do know it ought to be a lot of money because I think they are working short-handed. I strongly support those people who believe that there should be three officials. Two men just can't cover everything that's happening on the court. You have ten players out there, each trying to make his bones. Every one of them is—or ought to be—moving, hustling or working hard to hold or defend a position while simultaneously trying to outsmart the officials. Two pairs of eyes can't watch it all.

Sometimes when you see a coach blow up at the refs you're seeing the coach's considerable frustration with the game being taken out on the guys who might not have had anything to do with it—like a guy who has a bad day at the office and comes home and yells at his wife and kids.

I guess you'd call it misdirected anger, and that's what transpires occasionally between coaches and refs.

When a coach really loses his cool at courtside, it's because he sees the game and his team going down the tubes because of a bad call or the lack of a call.

There are lots of reasons for frustration in the world of professional sports.

My frustration almost blew me out of the Celtics organization at the end of the 1982 season.

The college draft was on. The Celtics were going to pick players in a phone/tv setup in the Blades and Board Restaurant in the Boston Garden.

The draft was held on a Monday. I spent the weekend playing golf in Indiana. When I walked into the draft meeting on Monday, one of the secretaries handed me a sheet of paper with a list of names on it and told me Bill wanted me to check off players' names on the list as they were drafted. I went back to the Celtics' offices.

Our secretary, Mildred Duggan, called me there and said Bill wanted me right back at the draft room.

By the way, Bill and I might disagree on some things but we'll both tell you that Mildred is a jewel. She's another person who makes the Celtics what they are.

I went back to the Blades and Boards and sat back down.

The draft was winding down. Most of the people had already left. Bill and Jimmy and maybe four or five people were still there. Bill picked up his briefcase and started out the door. He stopped and looked over at me. Then he crooked a finger at me and said, "Come here," like he was calling a dog. That's when the fuse started to burn. I walked over to Bill and as I did he started speaking to me in a very rough tone. Where had I been for draft meetings that were held over the weekend? He really let go at me.

Suddenly I lost it. I told him I had no part in any of this and he knew it. He'd made sure that I didn't know about or get asked to any meetings—ever. He'd made it clear to me that he didn't want me at any draft meetings or any other kind of meeting. To talk to me like this in front of other people was wrong.

Bill got hot and said some things.

I got hotter. The fuse hit the gunpowder. I did some things. We scuffled.

A friend of Bill's was there and she got very upset. I was still going after him as they hustled us out of the room.

Harry Mangurian's wife came up to me and spoke quietly.

"Is everything all right, K.C.?

I calmed down some. "Yeah," I said, "everything's o.k."

It wasn't.

I went back to the Celtics' offices. As I went past Bill's office he was standing just inside the door.

"I want to talk with you," he said.

I went in and closed the door.

Bill told me I was all through—finished—done.

I started after him again. I stopped. It was crazy. I was making a bad thing worse.

I left Bill's office and stood outside for a minute trying to find my lost cool. A couple of people were standing in office doorways staring at me.

I knew what I had to do.

I went down the corridor to Red's office. I wasn't looking for help. My thoughts were, "Well—no sense in not facing all the music right now. I'm not going to try and kid Red. I never have."

I told Red I had lost my temper and pushed Bill.

I know the world changes but Red doesn't. He listened and said, "You better call Harry and tell him. If we can help you get a job someplace else, we will. I'll be in touch with you."

I walked out of Red's office. Bill called down the corridor to me to come back to his office.

I thought, Oh Boy! What happens now? Bill closed the door and we stared at one another. He started to talk. He said he was sorry things had ended this way—that all this had happened.

We hugged.

I was confused. I felt as though somebody had punched me. I always thought Bill Fitch was a complicated guy.

I turned to leave.

Bill said, "K.C."

I looked at him.

He said, "If you ever shove me again understand that I'm going to shove you back."

I said, "O.K. Bill, that's fair."

I walked down the corridor from Bill's office. I looked at some pictures of some of my Celtics teams and teammates on the walls. I wondered if I'd ever see these offices again as I walked to the elevator.

All my rules about keeping my mouth shut and hanging on, always being a help and never a hindrance, paying whatever price is necessary to stay in the game, they had all blown up in my face.

As I started to think about all of my difficulties, both personal and professional, tears started to spill out of my eyes. They just came up and trickled down my cheeks. I couldn't stop them. When the elevator door opened I put my head down and hurried out of the building.

Chapter Seventeen

Well, despite all that happened, I still wondered about my status with the Celtics. During the summer at the basketball camp at Norwich I got a notice that Celtics' rookie camp would begin on such and such a day at Marshfield and that I was expected to be there.

When I arrived at Marshfield. Bill Fitch said hello—I said hello. Red said hello—everybody said hello. Nobody mentioned what happened at the end of the season. It was never mentioned by anyone.

That's not quite true. As time went on the players in their own different ways let me know they knew about the scuffle. I wasn't happy about that. I resolved that nobody could ever mark me down as giving a hint of having a problem with Bill.

Did Bill and I become arm and arm pals? No. He treated me just as he had before.

Basketball is like life. Sometimes it's crazy.

It was a tough year.

It was a strange season. Alternating Gerald Henderson and Danny Ainge at the one guard position was not easy for them and not easy for the coach, but they made it work.

The team played very well.

Still, the tension level seemed to grow and grow as the year went on. In the playoffs it came to a head.

Our series with Atlanta was very physical. Danny Ainge got hit with an elbow tossed by big Tree Rollins. It didn't quite take Danny's head off so he was able to tackle Rollins who then bit one of Danny's fingers very seriously while they were rolling around the floor. Danny had to have several stitches.

We beat Atlanta.

Our next stop was Milwaukee. Before we got there Don Nelson, the head coach, decided to tell the basketball fans of America that Danny Ainge was a vicious, dirty player and was a disgrace to the game. Whoa!

For the record Danny Ainge is as aggressive and scrappy a player as there is in the game of basketball. He will dive for the ball, throw himself through the air to intercept a pass, take the biggest man's charge — all without flinching. He would fight a rhino to win a game. He is not and never has been a dirty player. He would never try to hurt someone intentionally.

Competitive?

Mercy!

Someone said while he was playing soccer with his twelve year old nephew, Danny wouldn't let him get contact with the ball. Shut the kid out — totally.

The non-athletic side of Danny Ainge is a very religious one. Danny does not smoke or drink. Notice the victory scenes in the locker room. Danny is drinking Orange Crush. I'll bet the first thing the guys on the team would say — if they'd respond seriously to a question about Danny — would be that he is a super husband and father.

When we got to Milwaukee and they introduced Danny, the crowd went wild. Anytime Danny touched the ball or had his name mentioned they got themselves hoarse booing and screaming at him.

I guess Nellie was trying to psyche his team. Most of us will go a long way to win, but to resort to trying to destroy a player's reputation for a win is too far to go. Nellie's remarks about Danny showed a lack of professional class; they were untrue and he had to know it.

To show you how untrue things can stick, our general manager, Jan Volk, was having a conversation with the general manager of one of the top teams in the league, and the fellow said to him, shaking his head, "That Danny Ainge, what a bad actor. Imagine almost biting Tree Rollins' finger off."

That's as turned around as facts can get.

What happened in the Milwaukee series didn't happen because of the crowd or Nelly's psyche job. I wasn't a player and they're the only ones who really know, but the team lost it's synchronization. That was clear. I might explain what I think the reasons are but that's better left alone. The results are what the fans saw and still remember. Bucks 4–

Celtics 0.

Milwaukee swept us.

No player on that Celtics team will forget the fans out there waving the brooms at us. Somebody sold a lot of brooms in Milwaukee that spring.

I n the spring of 1983, Rick Robey and I were planning to open a little sandwich shop in the Quincy Marketplace. It was in that off time period between the end of the season and the beginning of basketball camps. We were hustling around town putting all the pieces of that project together.

Things were quiet with the Celtics. Harry Mangurian was in Florida, Red was in Washington.

Bill Fitch held a press conference in Red's office and announced he was leaving to become head coach of Houston. As far as I know, the announcement was a complete surprise to the Celtics family.

I forgot about the food business.

Ellen and I sat and talked and talked. Or I should say wondered and wondered. We wondered who would get the head coach's job and we wondered if whoever that was would keep me around.

It was a very unsettling time for us. After many conversations about being older parents of different backgrounds, Ellen and I had decided to have a baby. Now we hoped the baby's father would have a job.

The papers were full of talk and speculation about who was being considered for the job. Red asked me one day in the middle of a chat if I was interested in the job. I said, "Sure." Nothing more was said. I figured he asked me just to check off a list he probably had in his head.

"Is K.C. interested? O.K. we'll put him on the list that includes most of the coaches in basketball that are interested."

Did I think I would get the job? No. I didn't even think I was being seriously considered.

Red and Jimmy and I went out to Chicago in June to a free agents camp the NBA was running. It was a busy affair. Every free agent who could squeeze in the door was there working, running, sweating.

All the general managers and coaches were buzzing around. The Celtics head coaching job was a more discussed topic than who the most talented free agents were.

Red and I were going out to lunch with Jimmy Rodgers. Red asked me to stop by his room on the way to meet Jimmy in the lobby. When I walked in he said, "Are you still interested in the head coach's job?"

I said, "Yep."

That was it. We went to lunch and the three of us talked about the players at the camp. After lunch Red flew back home.

The next day was Saturday. The free agent camp wrapped up and I headed for the airport. When I walked on the plane the flight attendant said, "Congratulations, Mr. Jones."

I guess I nodded. I remember thinking, "What's that all about?" Another person said, "Good for you." I wondered who they thought I was.

People started coming toward me saying, "Congratulations." What was this?

One of them waved a Boston paper at me with big bold letters, KC JONES TO BE NAMED CELTICS COACH. My face must have lit up. I told them it was news to me. One of the flight attendants brought out champagne. The people wanted to toast me.

I said, "I'm not sure this is a fact."

They said, "Sure it is. The newspapers say the information came from a top Celtics' official."

So I said, "O.K. we'll toast. If it's wrong I'm toasting you, if it's right, you're toasting me."

I called Ellen as soon as the plane landed. She said the phone was ringing off the hook. I told her I didn't know if the news was fact or fiction so it might be best if neither of us said anything to the press. I asked her to pick me up and we'd drive up to the North Shore to the Georgetown Inn—a super little place that we liked where we could have dinner and hide from the press.

I called Red's house but there wasn't any answer. Ellen and I had a fine dinner and some finer talk about how strange life can be. The day before we were wondering if I'd hang on with the team—now we were wondering if I was the head coach.

I finally reached Red the next morning and asked him what was going on. He said, "The job is yours. Harry got talking with a sportswriter up in Boston and let the cat out of the bag before I had a chance to tell you. Let's have a press conference tomorrow and make it official."

I said, "Red, I don't have a contract. I don't know what the deal is."

"O.K. let's meet first thing tomorrow morning and get things settled then we'll have the press in the day after and wrap it up."

I wanted to get my thoughts clear. Being Head Coach of the Celtics had not been in my mind. I hadn't even signed a contract and I could feel a change in my life. I called my friend, Dr. Gus White, and went over to talk with him. I needed somebody with well-tuned ears to listen to me. Gus is a good listener.

Almost everyone in sports now uses an agent to negotiate contracts. So, did I pick up the phone and call my pal Willie Naulls and have him rush in from the Coast to deal with Red? Wow! I guess the right word for that would be *chutzpa*. I didn't even think about agents. I knew that if there was a list of the top fifty coaches in line for the Celtics job I was number one hundred and something. Agents can only help when you are in demand.

Red and I settled the financial aspects of our business very quickly. We talked about assistant coaches. We agreed that Jimmy Rodgers did a fine job. He wanted to stay and I wanted to keep him. Red suggested that I take Chris Ford as the number two man. Chris was getting ready to be an assistant at Boston College. I called him and we sat down at the 99 Restaurant near the Garden in the afternoon and talked. Chris lit up when I mentioned being an assistant with the team. I suggested that he think about it for a week or two, and that he might want to talk with Williams and anyone else in the NBA who could help in making a decision. Also, I told him to remember I might be a coach for only a year—or even a half a year. In this business, who knows.

At nine that night Chris called to say Boston College had given him permission to take the job.

I woke up earlier than usual the next morning, the day of the big press conference—the formal announcement that I was the Head Coach of the Boston Celtics.

I got up and walked around the apartment. We shared breakfast, then I got suited up and headed for the Garden. On the way I looked at my watch for the someteenth time. I was over an hour early.

Ellen and I were living in the North End at the time. We made some good friends there, like the Martignetti family. Their young son Anthony was my biggest fan. Later Mrs. Martignetti would care for Chris when Ellen returned to work. There is a playground on Atlantic Avenue just a couple of blocks from the Garden that overlooks the inner harbor and the *U.S.F. Constitution*—Old Ironsides. I walked over to the playground and sat on a bench. Some kids were playing ball, and they called out to me and waved, "Hey K.C.—Congratulations."

People going by called "Good luck." Some of the drivers in the slow-moving morning traffic honked their car horns and waved.

I sat watching the kids play ball. Thinking about them, I thought about my own kids. Divorce can do awful things to people and especially kids, but mine seemed to be doing alright.

I remembered hiking the hills of San Francisco with Ike Walker, McKinley Boyd and my high school idol, Charlie Boyd, looking for games at the playgrounds. It was sports that let us move around the toughest sections of the city. You could go anywhere, play with anybody of any color. The gangs never bothered you. You were somebody.

It was sports that opened doors for me and got me out of the trapped life at Double Rock.

I thought about Red and what he meant to my life. How he kept me when I was a rookie and he didn't have to. Now he was making me head coach when every coach in the country wanted the job. I thought about Russ and Satch and Dave Cowens who had been coaches before me. All good people. All had met with mixed success.

I could feel the tightness growing already. I knew how good the players were and I knew what good people they were. If the team stayed healthy they should win it all. With this team and these players the pressure would be on me. This would be like somebody giving me a great fortune and saying it was mine to use, but if I didn't spend it wisely it would all be taken away.

I have the finest research book in the world available to me. That's Red. He's an encyclopedia of basketball. I listen to him and take advantage of his knowledge.

From his first game in the league, Larry Bird has been what he'd been since I first scouted him in college. The most confident athlete I have ever seen.

The banners atop Boston Garden.

The 1985–1986 Boston Celtics NBA Champions.

Chapter Eighteen

Two days after I became head coach Jan Volk, our general manager, told me that the team could make a trade with the Phoenix Suns—Rick Robey for Dennis Johnson.
OUCH!

Jan Volk is a lawyer who has grown up in Celtics basketball. He's watched Red run the team since he was a youngster. He started at the bottom and knows every thing about what makes the Celtics' world turn. Jan has spent a long time in Red's shadow, but there will come a time when he will cast a great shadow of his own—although he probably won't bother since that isn't his style. The NBA has few general managers who do a great job. Jan is one of them. When it comes to making trades, we are all involved—the owners, Red, Jan, Jimmy, Chris. And in each situation we have all agreed. I have the final yes or no.

I knew that the trade would help the team in a big way. D.J. had the reputation of being a moody personality, but all I ever saw of him was a very intense competitor who got better when things got tougher. He was a complete player who had the potential to be a great star.

Rick Robey loved the Celtics. He is that kind of guy. His basketball skills were very underrated. He can become a dominant big man for an NBA team. With the Celtics, he was not going to get the chance to do that. Robert Parish and Kevin McHale would get most of the minutes. Phoenix would give Rick the opportunity to fill the big man's role.

The professional basketball truth was the Celtics needed Dennis. The human part of it was I was going to be very sad to see Rick go. I told Jan that I thought we should make the trade.

I called Rick and said, "Rick you've been traded to Phoenix."

I didn't know how else to handle it. It was like telling somebody about a death in the family—and that's what it felt like to me—but it was a basketball decision that had to be made.

After we jumped that first hurdle I talked about earlier, Dennis and I settled down. We got to understand and respect one another like a hand and glove.

Larry Bird says that Dennis Johnson is the best player he has ever played with. There is nothing anyone can say that can top that. Having Dennis and Larry on the floor is like having two coaches out there, and they have the same philosophy so it seldom stutters—it flows.

Dennis can watch individual players and sense the right defense. He's done it many times; he did it in the finals his first year against Magic. A wise coach will listen to a player like Dennis. I try to be a wise coach. During the Houston finals this year I talked seperately with both DJ and Robert to get their input on dealing with the Houston team.

Jan Volk was right in seeking the trade. Dennis Johnson has made everybody on the team more effective—including the coach. But making that trade was a hard way for the new coach to begin. It was quite an initiation back into the head coaching ranks.

I had gone from the fellow who uses the shovel to the man who owns the shovel. Sometimes that's not fun.

M.L. Carr told a friend of mine that he never saw anyone put as much pressure on himself as I did my first year as head coach. That's true. When I heard what M.L. said I was surprised because I thought the only person who knew how I felt inside was me, althought I shared some of those feelings with Ellen.

I felt that Red had gone out on a long, bending limb for me, and I was convinced that the limb would break if the team didn't win the championship. I didn't expect any chance at a second year. I certainly didn't want anyone else to know that.

I started our first practice by tossing a ball out and explaining what kind of drills I wanted to run that day. That was it. If I'd given a speech the players would have thought it wasn't me. We went right to work.

I'd gone seven years without being a head coach. I had to put my boss cap back on. I had to shape up my own system and ideas. The best way to do that is work not talk.

I had a good book of coaching knowledge to use. I saw my role as the man that gives direction—who is honest with the players and who knows his stuff. A large part of my approach to coaching young professional basketball players is to treat them like professionals. To give them a very large role. They're the talent. They have the creativity and imagination and these dynamic qualities must be allowed to come out.

M.L. said one day in early sessions, "Watch out Case, these guys' egos are as big as their salaries."

In some ways that's true, but so is their desire to play well and to win. They know the Boston Celtics are the best place in all of sports, in all the world, to be respected as an athlete.

I've always been proud to be associated with the Celtics. I'm proud of the people involved with the team. That includes the owners—Don Gaston, Alan Cohen and Paul Dupee. I've seen the bad times when Satch was stuck with an owner and players who were not in the Celtics tradition. It's back now and it's—MAH-VE-LOUS. The owners are eager, interested people. They are at ease with themselves, with the players, and with me. I enjoy their company. In a pressure-filled job, I have never once felt any pressure from them. Go around the league—and I've been around the league in more ways than one—you won't find better owners in sports. I have great respect for them.

When the team started the season and lost the first two games, the media jumped on me right away. Why wouldn't they? Great players with a new coach who was picked off the forgotten list. When the press kept after me about being concerned about opening the season with two losses I said I wasn't worried—not much. I tried to follow my rule about basketball: don't panic—think. I didn't panic but I was damn worried.

We held a long detailed practice and got ourselves in sync. The music started to flow very nicely.

I kept the door open for conversation with everybody and that means just that—and very definitely included the media. I think it's a pretty good rule for a coach to follow. Don't get too close to the players. Let them live their own lives but never be so far away from them that they can't come in and sit down and talk.

Any team with Larry on it will have the finest mixture of dedication and fun that a sports team can have. I guess you could say the Larry Bird recipe is total dedication and confidence mixed with wisdom and humor. He also shows great loyalty.

If Larry thinks people are ganging up on anybody, that man has a defender. Larry is like the gunfighter cowboy defending the underdog. He can set the team's tempo like nobody else. The rest of the team is right up there with him, ready to help.

Before a game one day in the Forum in Los Angeles, Bill Russell, who was announcing the game, was standing at mid-court talking with the great Jerry West who is now a Laker executive. Our guys were practicing very seriously. Then Larry said something that got them all laughing. Kevin McHale came over and said, "K.C., Larry said that's the first time you've been that close to Jerry West that you haven't yelled to Russell to help out."

One day in a tight game at halftime I was yakking away at the blackboard and pointing out first half mistakes on the video tape. It seemed to me the guys were all having mouth and face trouble. Their hands were rubbing around their lips and chins and cheeks. I was in the middle giving out the word from on high and started to walk to the other side of the blackboard.

I jolted to a stop and almost fell over. My shoe laces were tied together! Mister L. Bird was lying on the floor by my feet. That was the end of that halftime sermon.

In that first year before the playoffs I heard a rumor that some of the players were saying, "Win it for K.C."

What a compliment, I thought. They did win it. Was I proud of them! My mom came down from San Francisco to Los Angeles for a couple of games. We got blown out in the first game she saw. She told me she was going back home because she didn't want to see us lose to the great Laker team. She said it would hurt too much. That's the kind of Mom she is. What hurts me hurts her.

I was glad for the happy ending that year.

Something a lot more important than an NBA Championship happened during my first season as head coach. On October 18, 1983 our first child, my second son, Kent Christopher Jones was born.

I went to the hospital with Ellen and sat beside her during the delivery. She did not have an easy time. I was glad that I could be there with her. I didn't have the pain but I could feel it.

Christopher is a fine, active little boy. What more could we wish for?

The team had gone on a road trip, so after Chris came into the world and I was sure Ellen was alright I raced off to get a plane and join the team.

When Ellen woke up in the hospital bed there was a man standing at the foot of her bed with a present for the baby.

Mister Arnold "Red" Auerbach.

We would have had a better chance to win the Championship the next year if injuries hadn't hobbled us. All things considered, I thought we did very well, staying close to a great Lakers team. During the last half of the season, Larry played in the kind of pain that would have sent other people home to bed.

A healthy Max who could move and run would have been a great help in the playoffs. Not having that was too much for everyone else to carry.

I didn't have any nightmares when the thing was over. The guys did a hell of a job. I was disappointed for a day or so and then Ellen and Christopher and I went out and had a great summer.

Now we have a Bill Walton and a Jerry Sichting who can step in and do a lot of carrying when we need it. What a treat it is to look down the bench and see Bill and Jerry sitting there, totally into the game, as eager to play or cheer or help in any way as the youngest rookies in the league. Players like that make my sugarless gum taste sweeter.

Of course there are times for a coach when things are not sweet. If that happens when we're playing in the Garden, Ellen and I can settle in at home after the game and forget the rest of the world. If I'm on the road I like to go off somewhere by myself and have a good dinner and maybe sing a song.

The words and the music of some of my favorites really do seem to drive my troubles away. Song is good for what ails you—feeling bad, feeling good, it'll make you feel better. Song is a way to get out whatever is troubling you. The right word is always there. If the piano player starts on "Misty" or "San Francisco" or "Georgia" or "You're Nobody Til Somebody Loves You" or "It's Impossible"—he's got me right beside him with the words if he wants me.

I had that in mind one night in New York during my first year as head coach. We'd just lost a sixth game in the playoffs with the Knicks. We would be going back to Boston for a seventh game. We were not playing good defense. I was grim. I wanted to get away from it all for a while. I went out by myself and over to one of my favorite spots in New York, Jimmy Weston's on East 54th Street. Jimmy has good food and good music. I thought I'd have some of both and maybe sing a bit with the band. I knew that would take away the taste of the night's game.

Jimmy came over to me during dinner and asked me if I'd like to join him at a little party that was being held where there would be some music I might like. I said, "Sure."

We went uptown to what looked to me to be a private building. We went in and walked along a couple of corridors. Jimmy opened the door and we were in a room full of people having dinner. Sitting at the head table was the Chairman of the Board himself—Frank Sinatra.

He said, "Hi, K.C."

I shook hands and stood there kind of star struck. I hardly spoke. I was amazed Frank Sinatra knew who I was and I was so honored by it that I didn't talk. I wish I had said thank you to him for all the wonderful moments and memories he has given me through the years. His music has played all through my life. Good times and bad—Mr. Sinatra has made me feel better.

I'm glad to get a chance to say this—Thank you, Frank.

Well, we are running out of summer. It's about time to begin another season—and time to finish this book.

Some of the good feeling of winning another championship was washed away by the terrible news of Len Bias' death. What a waste—what a shame. The things that young man missed.

Ellen and I had a busy summer. I like to be on the go. I always have. That hasn't changed. Some other things have. I have become a bit of a public speaker. I'm not terrified when I stand up to speak. I enjoy it. People even pay me to do it—Imagine! The kid from Taylor, Texas who got sent home from school because he didn't begin to know how to read and write; the kid who had to sit in the back of the bus; who couldn't drink from a water fountain; or sit downstairs at the movies—that kid with his ears hanging down has become a man who feels good about himself.

Ellen and I traveled from the Swiss Alps to Las Vegas. People seem to know about the Celtics all over the world. It's strange, but when they see me folks all seem to have the same greeting.

They say, "Thank you, K.C."

Mercy!

That makes me feel so very good.

I've never been on one of those river rafting trips, but I suspect I feel like someone who has been through all the wild white water, who's bounced off the rocks and almost tipped over and drowned and then suddenly is gliding smoothly onto calm, peaceful water.

That's where I am now.

The future? I will hate to leave the Celtics but in a real way I never will. They're part of me. But the day will come and when it does I hope Ellen and I will still be in this house. She has made a wonderful home for us here and I think it's where we belong.

I'd like to give America a chance to taste my cooking. Not the whole country—just a dozen or so at a time. I'd like to have a small restaurant. A little horseshoe bar with a piano player. I could come out of the kitchen once in a while and sing a little.

There's a wild Frenchman on Nantucket—a Celtics fan—named Jean Berruet who has a great restaurant, the Chanticleer. He does it all—grows some of his food, catches the fish, has his fowl raised right on the island, then he cooks it to perfection.

It looks like a pretty good life to me.

So, if you're driving around the Boston area sometime in the future—when the basketball has stopped bouncing for me—and you see a little sign that says, "K.C.'s"—come on in. We'll yak a little and maybe the man at the piano will play us a song.

August 13, 1986

Bill Russell doing what he did best—retrieving the ball.

Danny Ainge leads the cheers.

Tommy Heinsohn displays his patented jump shot.

Larry Bird does it all, on defense and offense.

John Havlicek — one of the all-time great Celtics players.

The final series against Houston was a tough one.

Sam Jones—one of the greatest Celtics scorers.

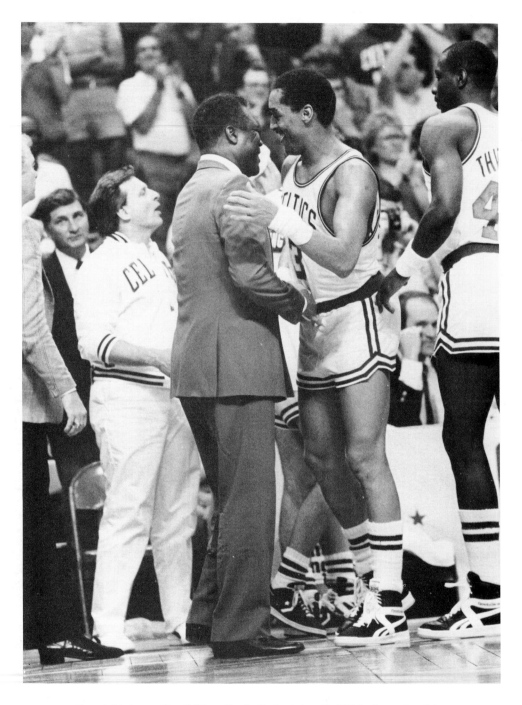

Sweet Sixteen—the Celtics clinch their sixteenth NBA championship.

One of the most satisfying days of my life—I was named head coach of the Boston Celtics.

Ellen and Christopher join me at a Massachusetts Special Olympics fashion show.